THE *Lyric* LIBRARY

Classic Rock

Complete Lyrics for 200 Songs

W9-CID-924

HAL•LEONARD

Other books in *The Lyric Library*:

Broadway Volume I
Broadway Volume II
Christmas
Contemporary Christian
Country
Early Rock 'n' Roll
Love Songs
Pop/Rock Ballads

ISBN 0-634-04350-1

Library of Congress cataloguing-in-publication data has been applied for.

Visit Hal Leonard Online at
www.halleonard.com

Preface

Songs have an uncanny ability to burrow deep into our gray matter, sometimes lying dormant for years or decades before something pings them back into our consciousness. All kinds of songs reside in there, more than we can count—not just songs we love and intentionally memorized and have sung again and again, but songs we once heard in passing, songs that form a soundtrack to significant people and places and moments in our lives, and even (or especially) songs that drive us crazy, like the chirping TV jingle that still won't let go years after the product it plugged has disappeared from the shelves.

Most of the time, though, our memories of songs are frustratingly incomplete unless we actively maintain them. The first verse and chorus that we blare out in the shower or at the jam session degenerates into mumbled lines, disconnected phrases, and bits and pieces inadvertently lifted from other songs. And, of course, there's the likelihood that what we *do* remember is riddled with mondegreens, or misheard lyrics. In these pages you'll find many opportunities to bring a little more completeness and accuracy to your rock repertoire, as well as to rediscover a nearly forgotten gem, wallow in nostalgia, or just browse through some prominent examples of the songwriter's craft.

Represented here are some of the Mount Rushmore figures of classic rock—The Beatles, The Rolling Stones, The Who, Eric Clapton—and many others who made their marks alongside and after them. In terms of songwriting, one of the most far-reaching changes of the '60s rock generation was the shift from performing tunes cranked out by prolific, professional songwriting teams—the Tin Pan Alley model—to writing their own material and aiming to elevate themselves from *entertainers* to *artists*. So in contrast to the early days of rock, many of these lyrics come from the pens (and, perhaps, bar napkins) of the same people who sang and played them to us.

For all the poetic ambition of a song like The Moody Blues' "Nights in White Satin," most of the selections here sing in simple everyday language about love (longing for it, finding it, losing it, ruing it), lust (aching with it, satisfying it, flaunting it), and revelry of all sorts. As the Stones put it, "I know it's only rock 'n' roll (but I like it)." Indulge, and enjoy.

Contents

Classic Rock

All Day and All of the Night

Words and Music by Ray Davies

recorded by The Kinks

I'm not content to be with you in the daytime.
Girl, I want to be with you all of the time.
The only time I feel all right is by your side.
Girl I want to be with you all the time.
All day and all of the night.
All day and all of the night.
All day and all of the night.

I believe that you and me last forever.
Oh yeah, all day and nighttime yours, leave me never.
The only time I feel all right is by your side.
Girl I want to be with you all of the time.
All day and all of the night.
All day and all of the night.

Repeat Verse 2

All day and all of the night.

All Right Now

Words and Music by Paul Rodgers and Andy Fraser

recorded by Free

There she stood in the street,
Smiling from her head to her feet.
I said, "Hey, what is this?"
Now baby, maybe maybe she's in need of a kiss.
I said, "Hey, what's your name, baby?
Maybe we can see things the same.
Now don't you wait or hesitate,
Let's move before they raise the parking rate."

Refrain:
All right now, baby,
It's all right now.
All right now, baby,
It's all right now.

I took her home to my place,
Watching ev'ry move on her face.
She said, "Look, what's your game, baby,
Are you tryin' to put me in shame?"
I said, "Slow, don't go so fast,
Don't you think that love can last?"
She said, "Love, Lord above,
Now you're tryin' to trick me in love."

Refrain

Allentown

Words and Music by Billy Joel

recorded by Billy Joel

Well we're living here in Allentown,
And they're closing all the factories down.
Out in Bethlehem they're killing time,
Filling out forms, standing in line.
Well our fathers fought the Second World War,
Spent their weekends on the Jersey shore,
Met our mothers in the U.S.O.;
Asked them to dance, danced with them slow.
And we're living here in Allentown,
But the restlessness was handed down.
And it's getting very hard to stay.

Well, we're waiting here in Allentown,
For the Pennsylvania we never found,
For the promises our teachers gave,
If we worked hard, if we behaved.
So the graduations hang on the wall,
But they never really helped us at all.
No they never taught us what was real,
Iron and coke and chromium steel.
And we're waiting here in Allentown,
But they've taken all the coal from the ground.
And the union people crawled away.

Every child had a pretty good shot
To get at least as far as their old man got,
But something happened on the way to that place.
They threw an American flag in our face.

Well I'm living here in Allentown
And it's hard to keep a good man down.
But I won't be getting up today.
And it's getting very hard to stay
And we're living here in Allentown.

Angie

Words and Music by Mick Jagger and Keith Richards

recorded by The Rolling Stones

Angie, Angie, when will those clouds all disappear?
Angie, Angie, where will it lead us from here?
With no loving in our souls and no money in our coats,
You can't say we're satisfied,
But Angie, Angie, you can't say we never tried.

Angie, you're beautiful, but ain't it time we said good-bye?
Angie, I still love you. Remember all those nights we cried?
All the dreams we held so close seemed to all go up in smoke.
Let me whisper in your ear;
Angie, Angie, where will it lead us from here?

Oh, Angie, don't you weep, all your kisses still taste sweet.
I hate that sadness in your eyes,
But Angie, Angie, ain't it time we said good-bye?
Oh, yes.

With no loving in our souls and no money in our coats,
You can't say we're satisfied,
But Angie, I still love you, baby.
Ev'rywhere I look I see your eyes.
There ain't a woman that comes close to you.
Come on, baby, dry your eyes.
But Angie, Angie, ain't it good to be alive?
Angie, Angie, they can't say we never tried.

Another Day in Paradise

Words and Music by Phil Collins

recorded by Phil Collins

She calls out to the man on the street,
"Sir can you help me?"
"It's cold and I've no where to sleep,
Is there somewhere you can tell me?"

He walks on, doesn't look back,
He pretends he can't hear her,
Starts to whistle as he crosses the street,
Seems embarrassed to be there.

Refrain:
Oh, think twice,
'Cause it's another day for you and me in paradise,
Oh, think twice,
'Cause it's another day for you,
You and me in paradise.
Think about it.

She calls out to the man on the street
He can see that she's been crying,
She got blisters on the soles of her feet,
She can't walk, but she's trying.

Refrain

Oh, Lord, is there nothing more anybody can do?
Oh, Lord there must be something you can say.

You can tell from the lines on her face,
You can see that she's been there.
Probably been moved on from every place,
'Cause she didn't fit in there.

Refrain

It's just another day for you and me, in paradise...

Another One Bites the Dust

Words and Music by John Deacon

recorded by Queen

Steve walks warily down the street
With the brim pulled way down low.
Ain't no sound but the sound of his feet;
Machine guns ready to go.
Are you ready, hey! Are you ready for this?
Are you hanging on the edge of your seat?
Out of the doorway the bullets rip
To the sound of the beat.

Refrain:
Another one bites the dust.
Another one bites the dust.
And another one gone,
  and another one gone.
Another one bites the dust.
Hey! I'm gonna get you too.
Another one bites the dust.

How do you think I'm going to get along
Without you when you're gone?
You took me for ev'rything that I had
And kicked me out on my own.
Are you happy? Are you satisfied?
How long can you stand the heat?
Out of the doorway the bullets rip
To the sound of the beat.

Refrain

Four Times:
Another one bites the dust.

There are plenty of ways that you can
  hurt a man
And bring him to the ground.
You can beat him, you can cheat him,
  you can treat him bad,
And leave him when he's down.
But I'm ready, yes, I'm ready for you.
I'm standing on my own two feet.
Out of the doorway the bullets rip
To the sound of the beat.

Refrain

Anytime

Words and Music by Robert Fleischman, Greg Rolie, Neal Schon, Roger Silver and Ross Vallory

recorded by Journey

Ooh, anytime that you want me.
Ooh, anytime that you need me.
Ooh, anytime that you want me to.
Ooh, anytime that you need me.

I'm standing here with my arms a mile wide.
I'm hoping and praying for you.
Listen to me and enlighten me, yeah.
I hope that you need me too, 'cause,

Ooh, anytime that you want me.
Ooh, anytime that you need me.

Give me all of your sunshine.
A spark is all I need
To take it away, all of the shadows.
Well, what more can I say?

Oh, anytime at all,
Anytime at all,
Anytime at all.

Repeat and Fade:
Ooh, anytime that you want me.
Ooh, anytime that you need me.
Ooh, anytime that you want me to.

Baby Grand

Words and Music by Billy Joel

recorded by Billy Joel and Ray Charles

Late at night, when it's dark and cold,
I reach out for someone to hold.
When I'm blue, when I'm lonely,
She comes through; she's the only one who can;
My baby grand is all I need.

In my time, I've wandered everywhere,
Around this world; she would always be there,
Any day, any hour;
All it takes is the power in my hands.
My baby grand's been good to me.

I've had friends, but they slipped away.
I've had fame, but it doesn't stay.
I've made fortunes, spent them fast enough.
As for women, they don't last with just one man;
My baby grand's gonna stand by me.

They say no one's gonna play this on the radio;
They said melancholy blues were dead and gone.
But only songs like these, played in minor keys,
Keep those memories holding on.

I've come far from the life I strayed in;
I've got scars from those dives I played in.
Now I'm home, and I'm weary in my bones;
Every dreary one-night stand,
My baby grand came home with me.
Ever since this gig began,
My baby grand's been good to me.

Baby, I Love Your Way

Words and Music by Peter Frampton

recorded by Peter Frampton

Shadows grow so long before my eyes,
And they're moving across the page.
Suddenly the day turns into night,
Far away from the city.
But don't hesitate 'cause your love won't wait.

Refrain:
Ooh, baby I love your way ev'ryday.
Wanna tell you I love your way ev'ryday.
Wanna be with you night and day.

Moon appears to shine and light the sky
With the help of some firefly.
Wonder how they have the pow'r to shine.
I can see them under the pine.
But don't hesitate 'cause your love won't wait.

Refrain

But don't hesitate 'cause your love won't wait.

I can see the sunset in your eyes
Brown and gray and blues besides.
Clouds are stalking islands in the sun,
Wish I could buy one out of season.
But don't hesitate 'cause your love won't wait.

Refrain Twice

Back in the Saddle

Words and Music by Steven Tyler and Joe Perry

recorded by Aerosmith

I'm back, I'm back in the saddle again.
I'm back, I'm back in the saddle again.

Ridin' into town alone
By the light of the moon,
I'm looking for old Sukie Jones,
She crazy horse saloon.
Barkeep, gimme a drink,
That's when she caught my eye,
She turned to gimme a wink
That'd make a grown man cry.

Refrain:
I'm back in the saddle again, I'm back.
I'm back in the saddle again, I'm back.

Come easy, go easy,
Alright till the risin' sun.
I'm callin' all the shots tonight,
I'm like a loaded gun.
Peelin' off my boots and chaps,
I'm saddle sore.
Four bits gets you time in the rack,
I scream for more.
Fool's gold out of their mine,
The girls are soakin' wet.
No tongue's drier than mine,
I'll come when I get back.

I'm back in the saddle again, I'm back.
I'm back in the saddle again.

I'm ridin', I'm loadin' up my pistol.
I'm ridin', I really got a fistful.
I'm ridin', I'm shinin' up my saddle.
I'm ridin', the snake is gonna rattle.

Refrain

Ridin' high.
Ridin' high.
Ridin' high.
Olé.
Got to, olé.

Back in the U.S.S.R.

Words and Music by John Lennon and Paul McCartney

recorded by The Beatles

Flew in from Miami Beach BOAC.
Didn't get to bed last night.
On the way the paper bag was on my knee.
Man I had a dreadful flight.

Refrain:
I'm back in the USSR.
You don't know how lucky you are boy,
Back in the USSR.

Been away so long I hardly knew the place.
Gee it's good to be back home.
Leave it till tomorrow to unpack my case.
Honey disconnect the phone.

Refrain

Back in the US, back in the US,
Back in the USSR.

Well the Ukraine girls really knock me out.
They leave the West behind.
And Moscow girls make me sing and shout.
That Georgia's always on my mind.

Refrain

Show me round your snow peaked mountains
    way down south.
Take me to your daddy's farm.
Let me hear your balalaikas ringing out.
Come and keep your comrade warm.

Refrain

Badge

Words and Music by Eric Clapton and George Harrison

recorded by Cream

Thinkin' 'bout the times you drove in my car.
Thinkin' that I might have drove you too far.
And I'm thinkin' 'bout the love that you laid on my table.

I told you not to wander 'round in the dark.
I told you 'bout the swans that live in the park.
Then I told you 'bout our kid. Now he's married to Mabel.

Yes, I told you that the light goes up and down.
Don't you notice how the wheel goes 'round.
And you better pick yourself up from the ground
Before they bring the curtain down.
Yes, before they bring the curtain down.

Talkin' 'bout a girl that looks quite like you.
She didn't have the time to wait in the queue.
She cried away her life since she fell off the cradle.

Bad Medicine

Words and Music by Desmond Child, Richie Sambora and Jon Bon Jovi

recorded by Bon Jovi

Refrain 1:
Your love is like bad medicine,
Bad medicine is what I need, whoa.
Shake it up just like bad medicine.

There ain't no doctor that can cure my disease.
I ain't got a fever, got a permanent disease,
And it'll take more than a doctor to prescribe a remedy.
I got lots of money but it isn't what I need;
Gonna take more than a shot to get this poison out of me.
And I got all the symptoms, count 'em 1,2,3.
First you need

Refrain 2:
(That's what you get for falling in love.)
Then you bleed,
(You get a little but it's never enough.)
On your knees,
(That's what you get for falling in love.)
Now this boy's addicted
'Cause your kiss is the drug, whoa.

Refrain 1

There ain't no doctor that can cure my disease.
Bad, bad, medicine.

I don't need no needle to be givin' me a thrill
And I don't need no anesthesia or a nurse to bring a pill.
I got a dirty down addiction that doesn't leave a track;
I got a jones for your affection like a monkey on my back.
There ain't no paramedic gonna save this heart attack.

Refrain 2

Refrain 1

There ain't no doctor that can cure my disease.
Bad, bad medicine is what I want.
Bad, bad medicine. Oh it's what I need.

I need a respirator 'cause I'm running out of breath.
You're an all night generator wrapped in stockings and a dress.
When you find your medicine you take what you can get.
'Cause if there's something better baby, well they haven't found it yet, whoa.

Refrain 1

There ain't no doctor that can cure my disease.

Refrain 1

Your love's the potions that cure my disease.
Bad, bad medicine, is what I want.
Bad, bad medicine.
Bad, bad medicine.

Ballroom Blitz

Words and Music by Mike Chapman and Nicky Chinn

recorded by Sweet

Oh, it's been getting so hard,
Living with the things you do to me.
My dreams are getting so strange.
I'd like to tell you ev'rything I see.
I see a man at the back, as a matter of fact.
His eyes are as red as the sun.
And a girl in the corner, let no one
    ignore her,
'Cause she thinks she's the passionate one.
Oh, yeah. It was like lightning,
Ev'rybody was fright'ning,
And the music was soothing,
And they all started grooving, yeah.
Yeah, yeah, yeah, yeah.

Refrain:
And the man at the back said, ev'ryone
    attack,
And it turned into a ballroom blitz.
And the girl in the corner said, boy,
    I wanna warn ya,
It'll turn into a ballroom blitz.
Ballroom blitz, ballroom blitz,
Ballroom blitz, ballroom blitz.

I'm reaching out for something;
Touching nothing's all I ever do.
I softly call you over.
When you appear there's nothing left of you.
Now the man at the back is ready to crack,
As he raises his hands to the sky.
And the girl in the corner is ev'ryone's
    mourner;
She could kill you with a wink of her eye.
Oh, yeah. It was electric,
So frightfully hectic,
And the band started leaping,
'Cause they all stopped breathing, yeah.
Yeah, yeah, yeah, yeah.

Refrain

Oh, yeah. It was like lightning,
Ev'rybody was fright'ning,
And the music was soothing,
And they all started grooving, yeah.
Yeah, yeah, yeah, yeah.

Refrain

Barracuda

Words and Music by Roger Fisher, Nancy Wilson, Ann Wilson and Michael Derosier

recorded by Heart

So this ain't the end, I saw you again today.
I had to turn my heart away.
Smile like the sun, kisses for ev'ryone,
And tales, it never fails.
You lying so low in the weeds.
I bet you gonna ambush me.
You'd have me down, down, down, down on my knees,
Now wouldn't ya, Barracuda?

Back over time, we were all trying for free.
You met the porpoise and me.
No right, no wrong, selling a song.
A name whisper game.
And if the real thing don't do the trick,
You better make up something quick.
You gonna burn, burn, burn burn to the wick,
Ooh, Barracuda.

"Sell me, sell you," the porpoise said.
Dive down deep to save my head.
You, I think you got the blues too.
All that night and all the next,
Swam without looking back.
Made for the western pools.
Silly fools, silly fools.

The real thing don't do the trick,
You better make up something quick.
You gonna burn, burn, burn, burn to the wick,
Oh, Barra, Barracuda.

Beast of Burden

Words and Music by Mick Jagger and Keith Richards

recorded by The Rolling Stones

I'll never be your beast of burden.
My back is broad but it's a-hurtin'.
All I want is for you to make love to me.

I'll never be your beast of burden.
I've walked for miles, my feet are hurtin'.
All I want is for you to make love to me.

Refrain:
Am I hard enough?
Am I rough enough?
Am I rich enough?
I'm not too blind to see.

I'll never be your beast of burden
So let' go home and draw the curtains
Music on the radio
Come on baby make sweet love to me

Refrain

Oh little sister, pretty, pretty, pretty, pretty girl
You're a pretty, pretty, pretty, pretty,
   pretty girl
Pretty, pretty, such a pretty, pretty, pretty girl
Come on baby please, please, please.

I'll tell ya
You can put me out
On the street.
Put me out
With no shoes on my feet
But, put me out, put me out,
Put me out of misery.

Yeah, all your sickness
I can suck it up.
Throw it at me
I can shrug it off.
There's one thing, baby
That I don't understand
You keep telling me
I ain't your kind of man.

Ain't I rough enough?
Ain't I tough enough?
Ain't I rich enough, in love enough?
Ooh! Ooh! Please

I'll never be your beast of burden.
I've walked for miles and my feet are hurtin'.
All I want is you to make love to me.

I don't need no beast of burden.
I need no fussin',
I need no nursin'.
Never, never, never, never, never, never,
   never, never be.

Bell Bottom Blues

Words and Music by Eric Clapton

recorded by Derek & The Dominos; Eric Clapton

Bell bottom blues, you made me cry.
I don't wanna lose this feelin'.
And if I could choose a place to die,
It would be in your arms.

Refrain:
Do you wanna see me crawl across the floor to you?
Do you wanna hear me beg you to take me back?
I'd gladly do it because
I don't want to fade away.
Give me one more day, please.
I don't want to fade away.
In your heart I want to stay.

It's all wrong, but it's alright,
The way that you treat me, baby.
Once I was strong, but I lost the fight;
You won't find a better loser.

Refrain Twice

Bell bottom blues, don't say good-bye.
We're surely gonna meet again.
And if we do, don't you be surprised
If you find me with another lover.

Refrain

The Bitch Is Back

Words and Music by Elton John and Bernie Taupin

recorded by Elton John

I was justified when I was five,
Raisin' cane, I spit in your eye.
Times are changin' now, the poor get far,
But the fever's gonna catch you when the bitch gets back.

Eat meat on Friday that's alright,
I even like steak on a Saturday night.
I can bitch the best at your social do's,
I get high in the evening sniffing pots of glue.

Refrain:
I'm a bitch, I'm a bitch, oh the bitch is back;
Stone cold sober as a matter of fact.
I can botch, I can bitch 'cause I'm better than you.
It's the way that I move and the things that I do, oh.

I entertain by picking brains,
Sell my soul by dropping names.
I don't like those!
My God what's that!
Oh, it's full of nasty habits when the bitch gets back.

Refrain

Bitch, bitch, the bitch is back.
Bitch, bitch, the bitch is back...

Blue Collar Man (Long Nights)

Words and Music by Tommy Shaw

recorded by Styx

Give me a job, give me security,
Give me a chance to survive.
I'm just a poor soul in the unemployment line.
My God, I'm hardly alive!
My mother and father, my wife and my friends,
You've seen them laugh in my face.
But I've got the power and I've got the will,
I'm not a charity case.
I'll take those long nights, impossible odds,
Keeping my eye on the keyhole.
If it takes all that to be just what I am,
Well, I'm gonna be a blue collar man.

Make me an offer that I can't refuse.
Make me respectable, man.
This is my last time in the unemployment line,
So like it or not,
I'll take those long nights, impossible odds,
Keeping my back to the wall.
If it takes all night to be just who I am,
Well, I'd rather be a blue collar man.

Keeping my mind on a better life,
Where happiness is only a heartbeat away.
Paradise, can it be all I heard it was?
I close my eyes and maybe I'm already there.
I'll take those long nights, impossible odds,
Keeping my back to the wall.
If it takes all night to be just what I am,
Well, I'd rather be a blue collar man.

Blue Sky

Words and Music by Dickey Betts

recorded by The Allman Brothers Band

Walk along the river,
Sweet lullaby.
It just keep on flowin',
It don't worry 'bout where it's goin', no, no.

Don't fly, mister bluebird,
I'm just walkin' down the road.
Early mornin' sunshine
Tell me all I need to know.

Refrain:
You're my blue sky,
You're my sunny day.
Lord, you know it makes me high
When you turn your love my way,
Turn your love my way, yeah.

Good old Sunday mornin',
Bells are ringin' ev'rywhere.
Goin' to Carolina,
It won't be long and I'll be there.

Refrain

Brain Damage

Words and Music by Roger Waters

recorded by Pink Floyd

The lunatic is on the grass.
The lunatic is on the grass,
Rememb'ring games and daisy chains and laughs.
Got to keep the loonies on the path.

The lunatic is in the hall.
The lunatics are in my hall.
The paper holds their folded faces to the floor.
And ev'ry day the paper boy brings more.

And if the dam breaks open many years too soon,
And if there is no room upon the hill,
And if your head explodes with dark forebodings too,
I'll see you on the dark side of the moon.

The lunatic is in my head.
The lunatic is in my head.
You raise the blade. You make the change.
You rearrange me till I'm sane.
You lock the door and throw away the key.
There's someone in my head, but it's not me.

And if the cloud bursts thunder in your ear,
You shout and no one seems to hear,
And if the band you're in starts playing diff'rent tunes,
I'll see you on the dark side of the moon.

Brass in Pocket

Words and Music by Chrissie Hynde and James Honeyman-Scott

recorded by The Pretenders

Got brass in pocket,
Got bottle, I'm gonna use it.
Intention, I feel inventive,
Gonna make you, make you, make you notice.

Got motion, restrained emotion.
Been driving, Detroit leaning.
No reason it seems so pleasing.
Gonna make you, make you, make you notice.

Refrain:
Gonna use my arms,
Gonna use my legs,
Gonna use my style,
Gonna use my side-step,
Gonna use my fingers.
Gonna use my, my, my imagination,
'Cause I gonna make you see
There's nobody else here, no one like me.
I'm special, so special.
I gotta have some of your attention, give it to me.

Got rhythm, I can't miss a beat.
I got new skank so reet.
Got something, I'm winking at you.
Gonna make you, make you, make you notice.

Refrain

Oh, oh, oh, and when you walk.

Breakdown

Words and Music by Tom Petty

recorded by Tom Petty and The Heartbreakers

It's all right if you love me.
It's all right if you don't.
I'm not afraid of you running away, honey.
I get the feeling you won't.

There is no sense in pretending.
Your eyes give you away.
Something inside you is feeling like I do.
We've said all there is to say. Baby,

Refrain:
Break down, go ahead and give it to me.
Break down, honey, take me through the night.
Break down, now I'm standin' here, can't you see?
Break down, it's all right,
It's all right, it's all right.

Repeat Refrain

Breathe

Words by Roger Waters
Music by Roger Waters, David Gilmour and Rick Wright

recorded by Pink Floyd

Breathe, breathe in the air.
Don't be afraid to care.
Leave, but don't leave me.
Look around, and choose your own ground.
For long you live and high you fly,
And smiles you'll give and tears you'll cry.
And all you touch and all you see
Is all your life will ever be

Run, rabbit, run.
Dig that hole, forget the sun,
And when, at last, the work is done,
Don't sit down, it's time to start another one.
For long you live and high you fly,
But only if you ride the tide.
And balanced on the biggest wave,
You race towards an early grave.

Bus Stop

Words and Music by Graham Gouldman

recorded by The Hollies

Bus stop, wet day, she's there, I say,
Please share my umbrella.
Bus stop, bus goes, she stays, love grows
Under my umbrella.
All that summer we enjoyed it,
Wind and rain and shine.
That umbrella, we employed it.
By August, she was mine.

Bridge:
Ev'ry morning I would see her waiting at the stop.
Sometimes she'd shop, and she would show me what she'd bought.
Other people stared as if we were both quite insane.
Someday my name and hers are going to be the same.

That's the way the whole thing started,
Silly, but it's true,
Thinking of a sweet romance
Beginning in that queue.
Came the sun, the ice was melting,
No more shelt'ring now.
Nice to think that that umbrella
Led me to a vow.

Repeat Bridge and Verse 2

But It's Alright

Words and Music by Jerome L. Jackson and Pierre Tubbs

recorded by J.J. Jackson

You don't know how I feel.
You'll never know how I feel.
When I needed you to come around,
You'd always try to put me down.
Well, I know, girl, believe me when I say
That you are surely, surely gonna pay.

Refrain:
Girl, but it's alright, alright, girl.
You keep hurtin' me, but it's alright.

Hey, now, one day you'll see
You'll never find a guy like me
Who'll love you right both day and night.
You'll never have to worry 'cause it's alright.
Oh, but I'm tellin' you, girl, and I know that it's true,
I wasn't made to love only you.

Refrain

Oh, oh, yeah,
My, my, my baby.
I said it's alright, alright, girl.
Hey, now, it's alright, alright, girl.

There's one thing I wanna say,
You'll meet a guy who'll make you pay,
Who will treat you bad and make you sad.
And you will ruin the love you had.
Oh, but I hate to say I told you so,
Baby, you got to reap what you sow.

Girl, but it's alright, alright, girl.
You are payin' now, but it's alright.
Good-bye, love, good-bye, girl.

California Girls

Words and Music by Brian Wilson and Mike Love

recorded by The Beach Boys

Well, east coast girls are hip,
I really dig those styles they wear;
And the southern girls with the way they talk,
They knock me out when I'm down there.
The midwest farmer's daughters
Really make you feel alright,
And northern girls, with the way they kiss,
They keep their boyfriends warm at night.

Refrain:
I wish they all could be California,
I wish they all could be California,
I wish they all could be California girls.

The west coast has the sunshine,
And the girls all get so tanned;
I dig a French bikini on Hawaii islands,
Dolls by a palm tree in the sand.
I been all around this great big world,
And I've seen all kinds of girls,
But I couldn't wait to get back in the States,
Back to the cutest girls in the world.

Refrain

Repeat and Fade:
I wish they all could be California...

Call Me the Breeze

Words and Music by John Cale

recorded by Lynyrd Skynyrd

They call me the breeze,
I keep blowin' down the road.
Well, now, they call me the breeze, baby,
I keep blowin' down the road.
I ain't got me nobody,
I don't carry me no load.

Ain't no change in the weather,
Ain't no changes in me.
There ain't no change in the weather,
Ain't no changes in me.
And I ain't hidin' from nobody,
Nobody's hidin' from me.

Well, I got that green light, baby,
I got to keep movin' on.
Well, I got that green light, baby,
I got to keep movin' on.
Well, I might go out to California,
Might go down to Georgia, I don't know.

Well, I dig you Georgia peaches,
Makes me feel right at home.
Well, I dig you Georgia peaches,
Makes me feel right at home.
But I don't love me no one woman,
So I can't stay in Georgia long.

Repeat Verse 1

Can't You See

Words and Music by Toy Caldwell

recorded by The Marshall Tucker Band

Gonna take a freight train down at the station, Lord.
I don't care where it goes.
Gonna climb a mountain, the highest mountain.
I jump off, nobody gonna know.

Refrain:
Can't you see, whoa, can't you see,
What that woman, Lord, she been doin' to me?
Can't you see, can't you see,
What that woman, Lord, she been doin' to me?

I'm gonna find me a hole in the wall,
I'm gonna crawl inside and die.
Come later now, a mean old woman, Lord,
Never told me good-bye.

Refrain

I'm gonna buy a ticket now, as far as I can.
Ain't never comin' back.
Grab me a south bound all the way to Georgia now,
Till the train, it run out of track.

Refrain Twice

I'm gonna take a freight train down at the station, Lord.
Ain't never comin' back.
Gonna ride me a south bound now, all the way to Georgia, Lord,
Till the train, it run out of track.

Carry On Wayward Son

Words and Music by Kerry Livgren

recorded by Kansas

Carry on my wayward son;
There'll be peace when you are done.
Lay your weary head to rest;
Don't you cry no more.

Once I rose above the noise and confusion
Just to get a glimpse beyond this illusion.
I was soaring ever higher,
But I flew too high.

Though my eyes could see, I still was
    a blind man.
Though my mind could think, I still was
    a mad man.
I hear voices when I'm dreaming.
I can hear them say:

Refrain:
Carry on my wayward son;
There'll be peace when you are done.
Lay your weary head to rest;
Don't you cry no more.

Masquerading as a man with a reason,
My charade is the event of the season.
And if I claim to be a wise man,
It surely means that I don't know.

On a stormy sea of moving emotion,
Tossed about, I'm like a ship on the ocean.
I set a course for winds of fortune,
But I hear the voices say:

Refrain

Carry on; you will always remember.
Carry on; nothing equals the splendor.
Now your life's no longer empty;
Surely heaven waits for you.

Repeat Refrain ad lib.

Caught Up in You

Words and Music by Frank Sullivan, Jim Peterik, Jeff Carlisi and Don Barnes

recorded by .38 Special

I never knew there'd come a day
When I'd be sayin' to you,
Don't let this good love slip away,
Now that we know that it's true.
Don't, don't you know the kind of man I am?
No, said I'd never fall in love again.
But it's real and the feeling comes
  shining through.

I'm so caught up in you, little girl,
And I never did suspect a thing.
So caught up in you, little girl,
That I never wanna get myself free.
And baby, it's true.
You're the one who caught me,
Baby, you taught me
How good it could be.

It took so long to change my mind.
I thought that love was a game.
I played around enough to find
No two are ever the same.
You made me realize the love I'd missed.
So hot, love I couldn't quite resist.
When it's right, the light just comes
  shining through.

Refrain:
I'm so caught up in you, little girl,
You're the one that's got me down
  on my knees.
So caught up in you, little girl,

That I never wanna get myself free.
And baby, it's true.
You're the one who caught me,
Baby, you taught me
How good it could be.

Fill your days and your nights,
No need to ever ask me twice, oh, no,
Whenever you want me.
And if ever comes a day
When you should turn and walk away,
  oh, no,
I can't live without you.
I'm so caught up in you.

And if ever comes a day
When you should turn and walk away,
  oh, no,
I can't live without you.

Refrain

Little girl, you're the one that's got me down
  on my knees.
So caught up in you, little girl,
That I never wanna get myself free.
And baby, it's true.
You're the one who caught me and
  taught me
And got me so caught up in you.

Centerfold

Written by Seth Justman

recorded by J. Geils Band

Does she walk? Does she talk?
Does she come complete?
My homeroom, homeroom angel,
Always pulled me from my seat.
She was pure like snowflakes;
No one could ever stain the memory of
   my angel,
Could never cause me pain.
The years go by,
I'm lookin' through a girlie magazine,
And there's my homeroom angel
On the pages in between.

Refrain:
My blood runs cold;
My memory has just been sold.
My angel is the centerfold.
Angel is the centerfold.
My blood runs cold;
My memory has just been sold.
Angel in the centerfold.

Slipped me notes under the desk
While I was thinkin' about her dress.
I was shy, I turned away
Before she caught my eye.

I was shakin' in my shoes
Whenever she flashed those baby blues.
Something had a hold on me,
When angel passed close by.
Those soft fuzzy sweaters too magical
   to touch!
To see her in that negligee is really just
   too much!

Refrain

It's okay, I understand,
This ain't no never, never land.
I hope that when this issue's gone,
I'll see you when your clothes are on.
Take your car, yes we will,
We'll take your car and drive it.
We'll take it to a motel room and take 'em
   off in private.
A part of me had been ripped,
The pages from my mind are stripped,
Ay no! I can't deny it.
Oh yeah, I guess I gotta buy it.

Refrain

Na na na na...

Changes

Words and Music by David Bowie

recorded by David Bowie

I still don't know what I was waiting for
And my time was running wild.
A million dead-end streets,
And ev'ry time I thought I'd got it made,
It seemed the taste was not so sweet.
So I turned myself to face me,
But I've never caught a glimpse
Of how the others must see the faker.
I'm much too fast to take that test.

(Ch-ch-ch-ch-changes) Turn and face the
    stranger.
(Ch-ch-changes) Don't want to be a richer
    man.
(Ch-ch-ch-ch-changes) Turn and face the
    stranger.
(Ch-ch-changes) Just gonna have to be a
    diff'rent man.
Time may change me, but I can't trace time.

I watch the ripples change their size,
But never leave the stream
Of warm impermanence.
And so the days flow through my eyes,
But still the days seem the same.
And these children that you spit on
As they try to change their worlds
Are immune to your consultations,
They're quite aware of what they're going
    through.

(Ch-ch-ch-ch-changes) Turn and face the
    stranger.
(Ch-ch-changes) Don't tell them to grow up
    and out of it.
(Ch-ch-ch-ch-changes) Turn and face the
    stranger.
(Ch-ch-changes) Where's your shame, you've
    left us up to our necks in it.
Time may change me, but you can't trace
    time.

Strange fascination, fascinating me.
Changes are taking the pace I'm going
    through.

(Ch-ch-ch-ch-changes) Turn and face the
    stranger.
(Ch-ch-changes) Oh, look out, you
    rock 'n' rollers.
(Ch-ch-ch-ch-changes) Turn and face the
    stranger.
(Ch-ch-changes) Pretty soon now you're
    gonna get older.
Time may change me, but I can't trace time.
I said that time may change me, but I can't
    trace time.

Cocaine

Words and Music by J.J. Cale

recorded by Eric Clapton

If you wanna hang out, you got to take her out; cocaine.
If you wanna get down, down on the ground; cocaine.
She don't lie, she don't lie, she don't lie; cocaine.

If you got bad news, you wanna kick them blues; cocaine.
When your day is done and you wanna run; cocaine.
She don't lie, she don't lie, she don't lie; cocaine.

If your thing is gone and you wanna ride on; cocaine.
Don't forget this fact: you can't get back; cocaine.
She don't lie, she don't lie, she don't lie; cocaine.

She don't lie, she don't lie, she don't lie; cocaine.

Cold as Ice

Words and Music by Mick Jones and Lou Gramm

recorded by Foreigner

You're as cold as ice.
You're willing to sacrifice our love.
You never take advice.
Someday you'll pay the price, I know.

Refrain:
I've seen it before, it happens all the time.
You're closing the door, you leave the world behind.
You're digging for gold, yet throwing away
A fortune in feelings, but someday you'll pay.

You're as cold as ice.
You're willing to sacrifice our love.
You want paradise,
But someday you'll pay the price, I know.

Refrain

(Cold as ice) You know that you are
(Cold as ice) As cold as ice to me.
(Cold as ice)

(Ooh, cold as, cold as ice)
You're as cold as ice,
Cold as ice, I know.
Yes, I know.

Come Sail Away

Words and Music by Dennis DeYoung

recorded by Styx

I'm sailing away.
Set an open course for the virgin sea.
'Cause I've got to be free,
Free to face the life that's ahead of me.
On board I'm the captain, so climb aboard.
We'll search for tomorrow on ev'ry shore,
And I'll try, oh Lord, I'll try to carry on.

I look to the sea.
Reflections in the waves spark my memory.
Some happy, some sad,
I think of childhood friends and the dreams we had.
We lived happily forever, so the story goes,
But somehow we missed out on the pot of gold.
But we'll try best that we can to carry on.

A gathering of angels appeared above my head.
They sang to me this song of hope, and this is what they said.
They said, "Come sail away, come sail away,
Come sail away with me, lads.
Come sail away, come sail away,
Come sail away with me.
Come sail away, come sail away,
Come sail away with me.
Come sail away, come sail away,
Come sail away with me."

I thought that they were angels, but to my surprise,
We climbed aboard their starship; we headed for the skies,
Singin', "Come sail away, come sail away,
Come sail away with me."

Come Together

Words and Music by John Lennon and Paul McCartney

recorded by The Beatles

Here come old flat top.
He come grooving up slowly.
He got joo joo eyeball.
He one holy roller.
He got hair down to his knee.
Got to be a joker he just do what you please.

He wear no shoe shine.
He got toe jam football.
He got monkey finger.
He shoot Coca-Cola.
He say I know you, you know me.
One thing I can tell you is you got to be free.
Come together right now over me.

He bag production.
He got walrus gumboot.
He got Ono sideboard.
He one spinal cracker.
He got feet down below his knee.
Hold you in his armchair you can feel his disease.
Come together right now over me.

He roller coaster.
He got early warning.
He got Muddy Water.
He one Mojo filter.
He say. "One and one and one is three."
Got to be good looking 'cause he so hard to see.
Come together right now over me.
Come together.

Cradle of Love

Words and Music by David Werner and Billy Idol

recorded by Billy Idol

Rock the cradle of love.
Rock the cradle of love.
Yes, the cradle of love don't rock easily, Sue,
Well, rock the cradle of love.
I rock the cradle of love.
Yes, the cradle of love don't rock easily,
    Sue, well, now.

It burned like a motor on fire
When the rebel took a little child bride to
    tease, yeah.
So go easy, yeah,
'Cause love cuts a million ways.
Shakes the devil when he missbehaves.
I ain't nobody's fool.
Come on, shake it up, whatever I do.

Rock the cradle of love.
Rock the cradle of love.
Yes, the cradle of love don't rock easily, Sue,
Sent from heaven above, that's right,
To rock the cradle of love.
Yes, the cradle of love, don't talk teasingly,
    Sue, yeah.

Pledge for your Romeo.
"Oh yeah, baby," I hear you moan, it's easy.
You know how to please me, yeah.
'Cause love starts my rollin' train.
You can't stop me. It ain't in vain.
I ain't nobody's fool.
Come on, shake it up, whatever I do.

These are the wages of love.
Rock the cradle.
These are the wages of love.
Rock the cradle.

Well, it burned like a motor on fire
When the rebel took a little child bride to
    tease, yeah.
You know how to please you, yeah.
Oh, my heart starts a rollin' train.
You can't stop me. It ain't in vain.
I ain't nobody's fool.
Come on, shake it up, whatever I do.

Rock the cradle of love.
Rock the cradle of love.
Sent from heaven above, that's right.
She rocked the cradle of love.
Rock the cradle of love, yeah.
Cradle of love. That's me, mama.
I'll rob the devil of love, alright.
Cradle of love.
(Rock the cradle of love. Cradle of love.)

Crazy Little Thing Called Love

Words and Music by Freddie Mercury

recorded by Queen

Verse 1:
This thing called love, I just can't handle it.
This thing, called love,
I must get 'round to it, I ain't ready.
Crazy little thing called love.

Verse 2:
A-this thing, (This thing.)
Called love, (Called love.)
It cries (Like a baby.) in a cradle all night.
It swings, (Oo.) it jives, (Oo.)
Shakes all over like a jelly fish,
I kinda like it.
Crazy little thing called love.

There goes my baby, she knows how to
     rock 'n' roll.
She drives me crazy, she gives me
     hot 'n' cold fever,
She leaves me in a cool, cool sweat.

Verse 3:
I've gotta be cool, relax,
Get hip, get on my tracks,
Take a back-seat, hitch-hike,
Take a long rise on my motor bike until
     I'm ready.
Crazy little thing called love.

Repeat Verse 3

A-this thing, called love,
I just can't handle it.
This thing, called love
I must get 'round to it,
I ain't ready.
Crazy little thing called love

Repeat and Fade:
Crazy little thing called love.

Crazy on You

Words and Music by Ann Wilson, Nancy Wilson and Roger Fisher

recorded by Heart

We may still have time, we may still get by.
Ev'ry time I think about it, I want to cry.
With bombs and the devil, and the kids
   keep comin'.
No way to breathe easy, no time to be young.
But I tell myself that I'm-a doin' all right.
There's nothin' left to do tonight
But go crazy on you. Crazy on you.
Let me go crazy, crazy on you, oh.

Your love is the evening breeze touching
   your skin.
The gentle, sweet singing of leaves in
   the wind.
The whisper that calls after you in the night
And kisses your ear in the early light.
And you don't need to wonder, you're
   doin' fine.
And my love, the pleasure's mine.
Let me go crazy on you. Crazy on you.
Let me go crazy, crazy on you, oh.

Wild man's world is crying in pain.
Whatcha gonna do when ev'rybody's insane?
So afraid of one who's so afraid of you.
Whatcha gonna do?

Oo, crazy on you. Crazy on you.
Let me go crazy, crazy on you.

I was a willow last night in a dream.
I bent down over a clear running stream.
I sang you a song that I heard up above,
And you kept me alive with your
   sweet flowing love.

Crazy. Yeah, crazy on you.
Let me go crazy, crazy on you, oh.
Crazy on you. Crazy on you.
Let me go crazy, crazy on you, yeah.
Crazy on you. Crazy on you.
Let me go crazy, crazy on you, oh.

Da Ya Think I'm Sexy

Words and Music by Rod Stewart and Carmine Appice

recorded by Rod Stewart

She sits alone, waiting for suggestions.
He's so nervous, avoiding all the questions.
His lips are dry, her heart is gently pounding.
Don't you just know exactly what they're thinking?

Refrain:
If you want my body and you think I'm sexy,
Come on, sugar, let me know.
If you really need me, just reach out and touch me.
Come on, honey, tell me so.

He's acting shy, looking for an answer.
"Come on, honey, let's spend the night together."
"Now, hold on a minute before we go much further.
Give me a dime so I can phone my mother."
They catch a cab to his high-rise apartment.
At last he can tell her exactly what his heart meant.

Refrain

His heart's beating like a drum,
'Cause at last he's got this girl home.
Relax, baby. Now we're all alone.

They wake at dawn, 'cause all the birds are singing.
Two total strangers, but that ain't what they're thinking.
Outside it's cold, misty, and it's raining.
They got each other. Neither one's complaining.
He says, "I'm sorry, but I'm out of milk and coffee."
"Never mind, sugar. We can watch the early movie."

Refrain

Day Tripper

Words and Music by John Lennon and Paul McCartney

recorded by The Beatles

Got a good reason for taking the easy way out.
Got a good reason for taking the easy way out, now.
She was a day tripper,
One way ticket, yeah,
It took me so long to find out, and I found out.

She's a big teaser, she took me half the way there.
She's a big teaser, she took me half the way there, now.
She was a day tripper,
One way ticket, yeah,
It took me so long to find out, and I found out.

Tried to please her, she only played one night stands,
Tried to please her, she only played one night stands, now,
She was a day tripper,
Sunday driver, yeah,
It took me so long to find out, and I found out.
Day tripper, yeah.

Don't Bring Me Down

Words and Music by Jeff Lynne

recorded by Electric Light Orchestra

You got me running, going out of my mind.
You got me thinking that I'm wasting
  my time.

Refrain:
Don't bring me down.
No, no, no, no, no. Oo, ee, hoo.
I'll tell you once more before I get off
  the floor.
Don't bring me down.

You want to stay out with your fancy friends.
I'm telling you it's got to be the end.

Refrain

Don't bring me down. Grrooss.
Don't bring me down. Grrooss.
Don't bring me down. Grrooss.
Don't bring me down.

What happened to the girl I used to know?
You let your mind out somewhere down
  the road.

Refrain

You're always talking 'bout your crazy nights.
One of these days you're gonna get it right.

Refrain

Don't bring me down. Grrooss.
Don't bring me down. Grrooss.
Don't bring me down. Grrooss.
Don't bring me down.

You're looking good, just like a snake in
  the grass.
One of these days you're gonna break
  your glass.

Refrain

You got me shaking, got me running away.
You got me crawling up to you ev'ry day.

Don't bring me down.
No, no, no, no, no. Oo, ee, hoo.
I'll tell you once more before I get off
  the floor.
Don't bring me down, down, down,
Down, down, down.
I'll tell you once more before I get off
  the floor.
Don't bring me down.

Don't Do Me Like That

Words and Music by Tom Petty

recorded by Tom Petty and The Heartbreakers

I was talkin' with a friend of mine,
Said a woman had hurt his pride.
Told him that she loved him so and
Turned around and let him go.
Then he said, "You better watch your step,
Or you're gonna get hurt yourself.
Someone's gonna tell you lies,
Cut you down to size."

Refrain 1:
Don't do me like that.
Don't do me like that.
What if I loved you, baby?
Don't do me like that.
Don't do me like that.
Don't do me like that.
Someday I might need you, baby.
Don't do me like that.

Listen, honey, can you see?
Baby, it would bury me
If you were in the public eye
Givin' someone else a try.
And you know you better watch your step
Or you're gonna get hurt yourself.
Someone's gonna tell you lies,
Cut you down to size.

Refrain 2:
Don't do me like that.
Don't do me like that.
What if I loved you, baby?
Don't, don't, don't, don't.
Don't do me like that.
Don't do me like that.
Someday I might need you, baby.
Don't do me like that.

'Cause somewhere deep down inside,
   someone is sayin',
"Love doesn't last that long."
I've had this feelin' inside night out and
   day in,
And baby, I can't take it no more.

Repeat Verse 2 and Refrain 2

Don't Fear the Reaper

Words and Music by Donald Roeser

recorded by Blue Öyster Cult

All our times have come.
Here but now they're gone.
Season don't fear the reaper,
Nor do the wind, the sun or the rain.
We can be like they are.
Come on baby, don't fear the reaper.
Baby take my hand.
Don't fear the reaper.
We'll be able to fly.
Don't fear the reaper.
Baby, I'm your man.
La, la...

Valentine is done.
Here but now they're gone.
Romeo and Juliet are together in eternity.
Forty thousand men and women every day.
Forty thousand men and women every day.
Another forty thousand coming every day.
Come on, baby.
Baby, take my hand.
We'll be able to fly.
Baby, I'm your man.
La, la, la...

Love of two is one.
Here but now they're gone.
Came the last night of sadness,
And it was clear she couldn't go on.
And the door was open and the wind
    appeared.
The candles blew and then disappeared.
The curtains flew and then appeared.

Said don't be afraid.
Come on baby. And she had no fear.
And she ran to him.
They looked backward and said goodbye.
She had taken his hand.
Come on, baby.
Don't fear the reaper.

Don't Let the Sun Go Down on Me

Words and Music by Elton John and Bernie Taupin

recorded by Elton John

I can't light
No more of your darkness.
All my pictures
Seem to fade to black and white.
I'm growing tired
And time stands still before me.
Frozen here,
On the ladder of my life.
Too late
To save myself from falling.
I took a chance
And hanged your way of life.
But you misread
My meaning when I met you.
Closed the door
And left me blinded by the light.

Don't let the sun go down on me.
Although I search myself,
It's always someone else I see.
I'd just allow a fragment of your life
To wander free.
But losing everything
Is like the sun going down on me.

I can't find
Oh the right romantic line.
But see me once
And see the way I feel.
Don't discard me
Just because you think I mean you harm.
But these cuts I have,
Oh, they need love
To help them heal.

Don't let the sun go down on me.
Although I search myself,
It's always someone else I see.
I'd just allow a fragment of your life
To wander free.
But losing everything
Is like the sun going down on me.

THE LYRIC LIBRARY

Don't Stand So Close to Me

Written and Composed by Sting

recorded by The Police

Young teacher, the subject of school girl fantasy.
She wants him so badly, knows what she wants to be.
Inside her there's longing.
The girl's an open page.
Books marking, she's so close now.
This girl is half his age.

Don't stand so, don't stand so close to me.

Her friends are so jealous: you know how bad girls get.
Sometimes it's not so easy to be the teacher's pet.
Temptation, frustration so bad it makes him cry.
Wet bus stop, she's waiting, his car is warm and dry.

Don't stand, don't stand so, don't stand so close to me.
Don't stand, don't stand so, don't stand so close to me.

Loose talk in the classroom, to hurt they try and try.
Strong words in the staff room, the accusations fly.
It's no use, he sees her. He starts to shake and cough
Just like the old man in that book by Nabokov.

Repeat and Fade:
Don't stand, don't stand so, don't stand so close to me.

Don't Stop

Words and Music by Christine McVie

recorded by Fleetwood Mac

If you wake up and don't want to smile;
If it takes just a little while,
Open your eyes and look at the day.
You'll see things in a diff'rent way.

Refrain:
Don't stop thinking about tomorrow.
Don't stop, it'll soon be here.
It'll be better than before,
Yesterday's gone, yesterday's gone.

Why not think about times to come
And not about the things that you've done.
If your life was bad to you,
Just think what tomorrow will do.

Refrain

All I want is to see you smile,
If it takes just a little while.
I know you don't believe that it's true.
I never meant any harm to you.

Refrain

Ooh, don't you look back.
Ooh, don't you look back.

Dream On

Words and Music by Steven Tyler

recorded by Aerosmith

Every time that I look in the mirror,
All these lines on my face gettin' clearer.
The past is gone; it went by like dusk to dawn.
Isn't that the way? Everybody's got their dues in life to pay.
I know nobody knows where it comes and where it goes.
I know it's everybody's sin;
You got to lose to know how to win.

Half my life's in books' written pages
Lived and learned from fools and from sages.
You know it's true,
All these things come back to you.
Sing with me, sing for the years,
Sing for the laughter 'n' sing for the tears.
Sing with me if it's just for today,
Maybe tomorrow the good Lord will take you away.

Twice:
Dream on, dream on, dream on,
Dream yourself a dream come true.

Dream on, dream on, dream on, dream on.
Dream on, dream on, dream on, ah.

Twice:
Sing with me, sing for the years,
Sing for the laughter 'n' sing for the tears.
Sing with me if it's just for today,
Maybe tomorrow the good Lord will take you away.

Dreamer

Words and Music by Rick Davies and Roger Hodgson

recorded by Supertramp

Dreamer, you know you are a dreamer.
Well, can you put your hands in your head,
  oh no.
I said dreamer, you're nothing but a
  dreamer,
Well, can you put your hands in your head,
  oh no.
I said far out, what a day, a year, a life it is.
You know, well, you know you had it
  coming to you.
Now there's not a lot I can do.

Dreamer, you stupid little dreamer,
So now you put your head in your hands,
  oh no.
I said far out, what a day, a year, a life it is.
You know, well, you know you had it
  coming to you.
Now there's not a lot I can do.

Work it out someday.
If I could see something (you can see
  anything you want, boy),
If I could be someone (you can be anyone,
  celebrate, boy),
Well, if I could do something (you can do
  something),
If I could do anything (can you do
  something out of this world).

We'll take a dream on a Sunday.
We'll take a life, take a holiday.
Take a lie, take a dreamer.
(Dream) dream (dream) dream
(Dream) dream (dream) dream along.

(Dreamer) Come on and dream and dream
  along.
Come on and dream and dream along (come
  along).
Come on and dream and dream along.
Come on and dream and dream along.

Dreamer, you know you are a dreamer.
Well, can you put your hands in your head,
  oh no.
I said dreamer, you're nothing but a
  dreamer,
Well, can you put your hands in your head,
  oh no.
Oh no.

Dreams

Words and Music by Stevie Nicks

recorded by Fleetwood Mac

Now, here you go again.
You say you want your freedom.
Well who am I to keep you down?
It's only right that you should play the way you feel it.
But listen carefully to the sound of your loneliness,
Like a heart-beat, drives you mad,
In the stillness of remembering what you had
And what you lost and what you had and what you lost.

Refrain:
Oh, thunder only happens when it's raining.
Players only love you when their playing.
Say, women, they will come and they will go.
When the rain washes you clean, you'll know.
You'll know.

Now, here I go again.
I see the crystal vision.
I keep my visions to myself.
It's only me who wants to wrap around your dreams.
And have you any dreams you'd like to sell.
Dreams of loneliness, like a heart-beat, drives you mad,
In the stillness of remembering what you had
And what you lost and what you had and what you lost.

Refrain

You will know.
Oh, you will know.

Drive My Car

Words and Music by John Lennon and Paul McCartney

recorded by The Beatles

Asked a girl what she wanted to be,
She said, baby can't you see?
I wanna be famous, a star of the screen,
But you can do something in between.

Refrain:
Baby, you can drive my car.
Yes, I'm gonna be a star.
Baby, you can drive my car and maybe I'll love you.

I told the girl that my prospects were good.
She said, baby, it's understood
Working for peanuts is all very fine,
But I can show you a better time.

Refrain

Beep beep mm, beep beep yeh!

Refrain

I told that girl I could start right away,
And she said, listen, babe, I've got something to say.
Got no car, and it's breaking my heart,
But I've found a driver and that's a start.

Refrain

Beep beep mm, beep beep yeh!

Dust in the Wind

Words and Music by Kerry Livgren

recorded by Kansas

I close my eyes
Only for a moment, and the moment's gone.
All my dreams
Pass before my eyes, a curiosity.
Dust in the wind.
All they are is dust in the wind.

Same old song.
Just a drop of water in an endless sea.
All we do
Crumbles to the ground though we refuse to see.
Dust in the wind.
All we are is dust in the wind.

Don't hang on.
Nothing lasts forever but the earth and sky.
It slips away.
All your money won't another minute buy.
Dust in the wind.
All we are is dust in the wind.
All we are is dust in the wind.
Dust in the wind.
Everything is dust in the wind.
Everything is dust in the wind.

Eight Miles High

Words and Music by Roger McGuinn, David Crosby and Gene Clark

recorded by The Byrds

Eight miles high and when you touch down,
You'll find that it's stranger than known.
Signs in the street that say where you're going
Are somewhere just being their own.

Nowhere is there warmth to be found
Among those afraid of losing their ground.
Rain gray town, known for its sound
In places small faces unbound.

'Round the squares, huddled in storms,
Some laughing, some just shapeless forms,
Sidewalk scenes and black limousines,
Some living, some standing alone.

867-5309/Jenny

Words and Music by Alex Call and James Keller

recorded by Tommy Tutone

Jenny, Jenny, who can I turn to.
You give me something I can hold onto.
I know you'll think I'm like the others before
Who saw your name and number on the wall.

Refrain:
Jenny, I've got your number,
I need to make you mine.
Jenny, don't change your number.
867-5309. 867-5309.
867-5309. 867-5309.

Jenny, Jenny, you're the girl for me.
You don't know me, but you make me so happy.
I tried to call you before, but I lost my nerve.
I tried my imagination, but I was disturbed.

Refrain

I got it (I got it), I got it,
I got your number on the wall.
I got it (I got it), I got it,
For a good time, for a good time call.

Refrain

Jenny, Jenny, who can I turn to.
867-5309.
For the price of a dime, I can always turn to you.
867-5309.
867-5309.

Emotional Rescue

Words and Music by Mick Jagger and Keith Richards

recorded by The Rolling Stones

Is there nothing I can say, nothing I can do
To change your mind?
I'm so in love with you.
You're too deep in, you can't get out.
You're just a poor girl in a rich man's house.
Oo oo oo...

Spoken:
Yeah, baby, I'm crying over you.

Don't you know promises were never
    meant to keep?
Just like the night, they dissolve up in sleep.

Refrain:
I'll be your savior, steadfast and true.
I'll come to your emotional rescue.
I'll come to your emotional rescue.
Oo oo oo...

Yeah, the other night, cry, cry, yeah,
    I'm crying.
Yes, I'm cryin', babe,
I'm like a child, babe.
Like a child, yeah, I was crying,
Crying like a child,

You think you're one of a special breed.
You think that you're his pet Pekinese.

Refrain

I was dreaming last night,
Last night I was dreaming, how you'd
    be mine.
But I was crying like a child,
Yeah, I was crying, like a child.
You will be mine, mine, mine, mine,
    mine, all mine.
You could be mine, could be mine,
    mine all mine.

I come to you so silent in the night,
So stealthy, so animal quiet.

Refrain

Yeah, you should be mine, mine, oo.

Repeat and Fade:
You will be mine, you will be mine, all mine.

Every Breath You Take

Written and Composed by Sting

recorded by The Police

Every breath you take,
Every move you make,
Every bond you break,
Every step you take,
I'll be watching you.
Every single day,
Every word you say,
Every game you play,
Every night you stay,
I'll be watching you.

Refrain:
Oh, can't you see
You belong to me.
How my poor heart aches
With every step you take.
Every move you make
Every vow you break,
Every smile you fake
Every claim you stake.
I'll be watching you.

Since you've been gone I been lost without a trace,
I dream at night I can only see your face.
I look around but it's you I can't replace,
I feel so cold and I long for your embrace.
I keep crying baby, baby please.

Refrain

Every move you make
Every step you take,
I'll be watching you.
I'll be watching you.

Every Little Thing She Does Is Magic

Written and Composed by Sting

recorded by The Police

Though I've tried before to tell her
Of the feelings I have for her in my heart,
Every time that I come near her
I just lose my nerve as I've done from the start.

Refrain:
Every little thing she does is magic,
Everything she does just turns me on.
Even though my life before was tragic,
Now I know my love for her goes on.

Do I have to tell the story
Of a thousand rainy days since we first met.
It's a big enough umbrella
But it's always me that ends up getting wet.

Refrain

I resolved to call her up a thousand times a day
And ask her if she'll marry me in some old-fashioned way.
But my silent fears have gripped me
Long before I reach the phone,
Long before my time has tripped me,
Must I always be alone?

Repeat Refrain and Fade

Evil Woman

Words and Music by Jeff Lynne

recorded by Electric Light Orchestra

You made a fool of me,
But them broken dreams have got to end.

Hey, woman, you got the blues,
'Cause you ain't got no one else to use.
There's an open road that leads nowhere,
So just make some miles between here
    and there.
There's a hole in my head where the
    rain comes in.
You took my body and played to win.
Ha, ha, woman, it's a cryin' shame,
But you ain't got nobody else to blame.

Refrain:
Evil woman.
Evil woman.
Evil woman.
Evil woman.

Rolled in from another town,
Hit some gold, too hard to settle down.
But a fool and his money soon go sep'rate
    ways,
And you found a fool lyin' in a daze.
Ha, ha, woman, what you gonna do,
You destroyed all the virtues that the Lord
    gave you.
It's so good that you're feelin' pain,
But you better get your face on board the
    very next train.

Refrain

Evil woman, how you done me wrong,
But now you're tryin' to wail a diff'rent song.
Ha, ha, funny, how you broke me up.
You made the wine, now you drink a cup.
I came runnin' ev'ry time you cried,
Thought I saw love smilin' in your eyes.
Ha, ha, very nice to know
That you ain't got no place left to go.

Refrain

Eye in the Sky

Words and Music by Alan Parsons and Eric Woolfson

recorded by Alan Parsons Project

Don't think sorry's easily said.
Don't try turning tables instead.
You've taken lots of chances before,
But I ain't gonna give any more.
Don't ask me, that's how it goes;
'Cause part of me knows what you're thinking.

Don't say words you're gonna regret.
Don't let the fire rush to your head.
I've heard the accusation before,
And I ain't gonna take it anymore.
Believe me, the sun in your eyes
Made some of the lies worth believing.

Refrain:
I am the eye in the sky,
Looking at you; I can read your mind.
I am the maker of rules
Dealing with fools, I can cheat you blind.
And I don't need to see anymore
To know that I can read your mind.

Don't leave false illusions behind.
Don't cry 'cause I ain't changing my mind.
So find another fool like before,
'Cause I ain't gonna take it anymore.
Believing some of the lies
While all of the signs are deceiving.

Refrain Twice

Eye of the Tiger

Words and Music by Frank Sullivan and Jim Peterik

recorded by Survivor
Theme from *Rocky III*

Risin' up, back on the street,
Did my time, took my chances.
Went the distance, now I'm back on my feet,
Just a man and his will to survive.

So many times, it happens too fast,
You change your passion for glory.
Don't lose your grip on the dreams
   of the past,
You must fight just to keep them alive.

Refrain:
It's the eye of the tiger,
It's the thrill of the fight,
Rising up to the challenge of our rival.
And the last known survivor
Stalks his prey in the night,
And he's watchin' us all
In the eye of the tiger.

Face to face out in the heat,
Hangin' tough, stayin' hungry.
They stack the odds, still we take to the
   street
For the kill with the skill to survive.

Refrain

Risin' up, straight to the top,
Had guts, got the glory.
Went the distance, now I'm not gonna stop,
Just a man and his will to survive.

Refrain

Four Times:
The eye of the tiger.

Fame

Words and Music by John Lennon, David Bowie and Carlos Alomar

recorded by David Bowie

Fame makes a man take things over.
Fame lets him loose, hard to swallow.
Fame puts you there where things are hollow. Fame.
Fame, it's not your brain, it's just the flame
That burns your change to keep you insane. Fame.

Fame, what you like is in the limo.
Fame, what you get is no tomorrow.
Fame, what you need you have to borrow. Fame.
Fame, it's mine, it's mine, it's just his line
To bind your time, it drives you to crime. Fame.

Is it any wonder I reject you first?
Fame, fame, fame, fame.
Is it any wonder you are too cool to fool? Fame.
Fame, bully for you, chilly for me,
Got to get a rain check on pain. Fame.

Fame, fame,
Fame, fame,
Fame, fame, fame,
Fame, fame, fame, fame,
Fame, fame, fame, fame,
Fame, fame, fame,
Fame, what's your name?

Fooling Yourself (The Angry Young Man)

Words and Music by Tommy Shaw

recorded by Styx

Spoken:
Relax, take it easy.

You see the world through your cynical eyes;
You're a troubled young man, I can tell.
You've got it all in the palm of your hand,
But your hand's wet with sweat, and your head needs a rest.

And you're fooling yourself if you don't believe it.
You're kidding yourself if you don't believe it.
Why must you be such an angry young man
When your future looks quite bright to me?
And how can there be such a sinister plan
That could hide such a lamb, such a caring young man?

And you're fooling yourself if you don't believe it.
You're killing yourself if you don't believe it.
Get up! (Get up!) Get back on your feet.
You're the one they can't beat and you know it.
Come on! (Come on!) Let's see what you've got.
Just take your best shot and don't blow it.

You're fooling yourself if you don't believe it.
You're killing yourself if you don't believe it.
Get up! (Get up!) Get back on your feet.
You're the one they can't beat and you know it.
Come on! (Come on!) Let's see what you've got.
Just take your best shot and don't blow it.

For Your Love

Words and Music by Graham Gouldman

recorded by The Yardbirds

For your love.
For your love.
For your love.
I'd give you everything and more and that's for sure.
(For your love.)
I'd give you diamond rings and things right to your door.
(For your love.)

Refrain:
To thrill you with delight,
I'd give you diamonds bright.
There'll be things that will excite,
To make you dream of me at night.
For your love,
For your love.

For your love.
For your love.
I'd give the moon if it were mine to give.
(For your love.)
I'd give that star and the sun above 'fore I live.
(For your love.)

Refrain

For your love,
For your love.
I would give you the stars above.
For your love,
For your love.
I would give you all I could.

Repeat Verse 1 and Refrain

For your love,
For your love.

Forever Young

Words and Music by Rod Stewart, Jim Cregan, Kevin Savigar and Bob Dylan

recorded by Rod Stewart

May the good Lord be with you
Down every road you roam.
And may sunshine and happiness
Surround you when you're far from home.

And may you grow to be proud,
Dignified and true.
And do unto others
As you'd have done to you.
Be courageous and be brave.
And in my heart you'll always stay

Refrain:
Forever young,
Forever young,
Forever young,
Forever young.

May good fortune be with you,
May your guiding light be strong,
Build a stairway to heaven
With a prince or a vagabond.
And may you never love in vain.
And in my heart you will remain

Refrain

Forever young,
Forever young.

And when you finally fly away,
I'll be hoping that I served you well.
For all the wisdom of a lifetime,
No one can ever tell.
But whatever road you choose,
I'm right behind you, win or lose.

Refrain

Forever young,
Forever young,
Forever young,
Forever young.

Fortress Around Your Heart

Written and Composed by G.M. Sumner

recorded by Sting

Under the ruins of a walled city,
Crumbling towers in beams of yellow light.
No flags of truce, no cries of pity;
The siege guns had been pounding through
   the night.
It took a day to build the city.
We walked through its streets in the
   afternoon.
As I returned across the fields I'd known,
I recognized the walls that I once made.
Had to stop in my tracks for fear
Of walking on the mines I'd laid.

Refrain:
And if I've built this fortress around your
   heart,
Encircled you in trenches and barbed wire,
Then let me build a bridge,
For I cannot fill the chasm,
And let me set the battlements on fire.

Then I went off to fight some battle
That I'd invented inside my head.
Away so long for years and years,
You probably thought or even wished that I
   was dead.
While the armies are all sleeping
Beneath the tattered flag we'd made,
I had to stop in my tracks for fear
Of walking on the mines I'd laid.

Refrain

This prison has now become your home,
A sentence you seem prepared to pay.
It took a day to build the city.
We walked through its streets in the
   afternoon,
As I returned across the lands I'd known,
I recognized the fields where I once played.
I had to stop in my tracks for fear
Of walking on the mines I'd laid.

Refrain

Free Ride

Words and Music by Dan Hartman

recorded by Edgar Winter Group

The mountain is high, the valley is low,
And you're confused on which way to go.
So I've come here to give you a hand
And lead you into the promised land.

Refrain:
So, come on and take a free ride,
(Free ride.)
Come on and sit here by my side.
Come on and take a free ride.

All over this country I've seen it the same;
Nobody's winning at this kind of game.
We've gotta do better, it's time to begin.
You know all the answers must come from within.

Refrain Twice

Come on and take a free ride.
Yeah, yeah, yeah, yeah.
Come on and take a free ride...

Give a Little Bit

Words and Music by Rick Davies and Roger Hodgson

recorded by Supertramp

Give a little bit,
Give a little bit of your love to me.
I'll give a little bit,
I'll give a little bit of my love to you.
There's so much that we need to share,
So send a smile and show you care.

I'll give a little bit,
I'll give a little bit of my life for you.
So, give a little bit,
Oh, give a little bit of your time to me.
See the man with the lonely eyes?
Oh, take his hand, you'll be surprised.

Give a little bit,
Give a little bit of your love to me.
I'll give a little bit,
I'll give a little bit of my life for you.
Now's the time that we need to share,
So find yourself, we're on our way back home.
Oh, goin' home.
Don't you need, don't you need to feel at home.
Oh, yeah, we gotta sing.

Gloria

Words and Music by Van Morrison

recorded by Them; The Shadows of Knight

Like to tell you 'bout my baby.
You know she comes 'round
Just 'bout five feet four
From her head to the ground.
Well, she comes around here
Just about midnight.
She makes me feel so good, Lord,
Makes me feel alright.

Refrain:
Her name is G L O R I A.
G L O R I A (Gloria),
G L O R I A (Gloria),
G L O R I A (Gloria),
Alright one time (Gloria, Gloria).

Yeah, she comes around here,
Just about midnight.
Makes me feel so good, Lord,
Makes me feel alright.
Walkin' down on the street,
Comes up to my house.
She knocks upon my door,
Makes me feel alright.

Refrain

Godzilla

Words and Music by Donald Roeser

recorded by Blue Öyster Cult

With a purposeful grimace and a terrible sound,
He pulls the spinning high-tension wires down.
Helpless people on subway trains
Scream bug-eyed as he looks in on them.
He picks up a bus and he throws it back down,
As he wades through the buildings toward the center of town.

Refrain (Three Times):
Oh, no, they say he's got to go.
Go, go, Godzilla. Whoo.
Oh, no, there goes Toyko.
Go, go, Godzilla. Whoo.

Four Times:
History shows again and again
How nature points out the folly of man.
Godzilla.

Green-Eyed Lady

Words and Music by Jerry Corbetta, J.C. Phillips and David Riordan

recorded by Sugarloaf

Green-eyed lady, lovely lady.
Strolling slowly towards the sun.
Green-eyed lady, ocean lady.
Soothing every raging wave that comes.

Refrain:
Green-eyed lady passions lady.
Dressed in love, she lives for life to be.
Green-eyed lady feels life, I never see,
Setting suns and lovely lovers free.

Green-eyed lady, wind swept lady.
Rules the night, the waves, the sand.
Green-eyed lady, ocean lady.
Child of nature, friend of man.

Refrain

Hair of the Dog

Words and Music by Dan McCafferty, Darrell Sweet, Pete Agnew and Manuel Charlton

recorded by Nazareth

I'll break the soul shaker.
I've been told about you.
She rode up, then I showed her,
What they've been sayin' must be true.

Refrain:
Red hot mama, love that charmer;
Just got to pay your dues.
Now you're messin' with a, a son of a bitch.
Now you're messin' with a son of a bitch.
Now you're messin' with a son of a bitch.
Now you're messin' with a son of a bitch.

Talkin' to her with poison ivy,
You ain't gonna cling to me.
Man taker, bone finger,
I ain't so blind I can't see.

Refrain

Now you're messin' with a, a son of a bitch.
Now you're messin' with a son of a bitch.
Now you're messin' with a son of a bitch.
Now you're messin' with a son of a bitch.

Happy

Words and Music by Mick Jagger and Keith Richards

recorded by The Rolling Stones

Well, I never kept a dollar past sunset;
Always burned a hole in my pants.
Never made a school mama happy;
Never blew a second chance on love.
I need a love to keep me happy,
I need a love to keep me happy.
Baby, baby, keep me happy.
Baby, baby, keep me happy.

Always took candy from strangers;
Didn't wanna get me no trade.
Never want to be like Papa,
Workin' for the boss ev'ry night and day.
I need a love to keep me happy.
I need a love, baby, won't ya keep me
Happy? Baby, won't ya keep me happy?
Baby, please keep me.

I need a love to keep me happy,
I need a love to keep me happy.
Baby, baby, keep me happy.
Baby.

Never got a flash out of cocktails
When I got some flesh off the bone.
Never got a lift out of Lear jet
When I can fly way back home.
I need a love to keep me happy,
I need a love to keep me happy.
Baby, baby, keep me happy.
Baby, baby, keep me happy.
Baby.

Happy, baby, won't ya keep me happy?
Baby, won't ya keep me happy?
Baby, won't you keep me happy?
Baby, won't you keep me happy?

A Hard Day's Night

Words and Music by John Lennon and Paul McCartney

recorded by The Beatles
from the film *A Hard Day's Night*

Refrain:
It's been a hard day's night,
And I've been working like a dog.
It's been a hard day's night,
I should be sleeping like a log.
But when I get home to you,
I find the things that you do
Will make me feel alright.

You know I work all day,
To get you money to buy you things.
And it's worth it just to hear you say,
You're gonna give me everything.
So why on earth should I moan,
'Cause when I get you alone,
You know I feel okay.

When I'm home
Everything seems to be right.
When I'm home,
Feeling you holding me tight, tight, yeah.

Refrain

So why on earth should I moan,
'Cause when I get you alone,
You know I feel okay.

When I'm home
Everything seems to be right.
When I'm home,
Feeling you holding me tight, tight, yeah.

Refrain

Heart and Soul

Words and Music by Mike Chapman and Nicky Chinn

recorded by Huey Lewis and The News

Two o'clock this morning
If she should come a calling
I wouldn't dream of turning her away.
And if it got hot and hectic
I know she'd be electric.
I'd let her take her chances with me.
You see, she gets what she wants

'Cause she's heart and soul.
She's hot and cold.
She's got it all.
Hot loving ev'ry night.

Well, can't you see her standing there?
See how she looks, see how she cares.
I let her steal the night away from me.
Nine o'clock this morning
She left without a warning.
I let her take advantage of me.
You see, she got what she wanted

'Cause she's heart and soul
She's hot and cold
She's got it all.
Hot loving every night

The Heart of the Matter

Words and Music by John David Souther, Don Henley and Mike Campbell

recorded by Don Henley

I got the call today, I didn't want to hear,
But I knew that it would come.
An old, true friend of ours was talkin' on the phone,
She said you found someone.
And I thought of all the bad luck and the struggles we went through
And how I lost me and you lost you.
What are those voices outside love's open door
Makes us throw off our contentment and beg for something more?
I'm learning to live without you now,
But I miss you sometimes.
The more I know, the less I understand.
All the things I thought I knew, I'm learning again.

I've been trying to get down to the heart of the matter,
But my will gets weak and my thoughts seem to scatter.
But I think it's about forgiveness, forgiveness.
Even if, even if you don't love me anymore.

Ah, these times are so uncertain,
There's a yearning undefined...people filled with rage.
We all need a little tenderness.
How can love survive in such a graceless age?
The trust and self-assurance that led to happiness,
They're the very things we kill, I guess.
Pride and competition cannot fill these empty arms,
And the work I put between us doesn't keep me warm.
I'm learning to live without you now,
But I miss you, baby.
The more I know, the less I understand.
All the things I thought I'd figured out, I have to learn again.

I've been trying to get down to the heart of the matter,
But everything changes, and my friends seem to scatter.
But I think it's about forgiveness, forgiveness.
Even if, even if you don't love me anymore.

There are people in your life who've come and gone,
They let you down, you know they've hurt your pride.
You better put it all behind you 'cause life goes on.
You keep carryin' that anger, it'll eat you up inside, baby.

I've been trying to get down to the heart of the matter,
But my will gets weak and my thoughts seem to scatter.
But I think it's about forgiveness, forgiveness.
Even if, even if you don't love me.

I've been tryin' to get down to the heart of the matter,
Because the flesh will get weak and the ashes will scatter.
So I'm thinkin' about forgiveness, forgiveness.
Even if, even if you don't love me.

Heartache Tonight

Words and Music by John David Souther, Don Henley, Glenn Frey and Bob Seger

recorded by The Eagles

Somebody's gonna hurt someone
Before the night is through.
Somebody's gonna come undone;
There's nothin' we can do.
Everybody wants to touch somebody,
If it takes all night.
Everybody wants to take a little chance,
Make it come out right.
There's gonna be a heartache tonight,
A heartache tonight, I know.
Lord, I know.

Some people like to stay out late.
Some folks can't hold out that long.
But nobody wants to go home now;
There's too much goin' on.
The night is gonna last forever.
Last all, last all summer long.
Sometime before the sun comes up
The radio is gonna play that song.
There's gonna be a heartache tonight,
A heartache tonight, I know.

There's gonna be a heartache tonight,
A heartache tonight, I know.
Lord, I know.
There's gonna be a heartache tonight,
The moon's shinin' bright,
So turn out the light, and we'll get it right.
There's gonna be a heartache tonight,
A heartache tonight, I know.

Somebody's gonna hurt someone
Before the night is through.
Somebody's gonna come undone;
There's nothin' we can do.
Everybody wants to touch somebody,
If it takes all night.
Everybody wants to take a little chance,
Make it come out right.
There's gonna be a heartache tonight,
A heartache tonight, I know.

Let's go.
We can beat around the bushes;
We can get down to the bone;
We can leave it in the parkin' lot,
But either way, there's gonna be a heartache
    tonight,
A heartache tonight, I know.
Oh, I know.
There'll be a heartache tonight,
A heartache tonight, I know.

Heat of the Moment

Words and Music by Geoffrey Downes and John Wetton

recorded by Asia

I never meant to be so bad to you.
One thing I said that I would never do.
A look from you and I would fall from grace.
And that would wipe the smile right from
   my face.

Do you remember when we used to dance?
And incidents arose from circumstance.
One thing led to another, we were young.
And we would scream together
   songs unsung.

It was the heat of the moment,
Tellin' you what my heart meant.
The heat of the moment showed in
   your eyes.

And now you find yourself in '82.
The disco huff was on the charm for you.
You can concern yourself with bigger things.
You catch a pearl and ride the
   dragon's wings.

'Cause it's the heat of the moment.
Heat of the moment.
The heat of the moment showed in
   your eyes.

And when your looks are gone and
   you're alone,
How many nights you sit beside the phone.
What were the things you wanted for
   yourself?
Teenage ambitions you remember well.

It was the heat of the moment
Tellin' you what your heart meant.
The heat of the moment showed in
   your eyes.
It was the heat of the moment.
Heat of the moment.
The heat of the moment showed in
   your eyes.

Heaven

Words and Music by Bryan Adams and Jim Vallance

recorded by Bryan Adams

Oh, thinkin' about all our younger years.
There was only you and me,
We were young and wild and free.
Now nothin' can take you away from me.
We've been down that road before,
But that's over now, you keep me comin' back for more.

Refrain:
Baby, you're all that I want
When you're lyin' here in my arms.
I'm findin' it hard to believe we're in heaven.
And love is all that I need,
And I found it there in your heart.
It isn't too hard to see we're in heaven.

Oh, once in your life you find someone
Who will turn your world around,
Bring you up when you're feelin' down.
Yeah, nothin' could change what you mean to me.
Oh, there's lots that I could say,
But just hold me now, 'cause our love will light the way.

Refrain

I've been waitin' for so long
For somethin' to arrive,
For love to come along.
Now our dreams are comin' true.
Through the good times and the bad,
Yeah, I'll be standin' there by you.

Refrain

Heaven.
You're all that I want, you're all that I need.

Hello, It's Me

Words and Music by Todd Rundgren

recorded by Todd Rundgren

Hello, it's me, I've thought about us for a long, long time.
Maybe I think too much but something's wrong.
There's something here that doesn't last too long.
Maybe I shouldn't think of you as mine.

Seeing you, or seeing anything as much as I do,
I take for granted that you're always there.
I take for granted that you just don't care.
Sometimes I can't help seeing all the way through.

Refrain:
It's important to me that you know you are free,
'Cause I never want to make you change for me.
Think of me.
You know that I'd be with you if I could.
I'll come around to see you once in awhile,
Or if I ever need a reason to smile,
And spend the night if you think I should.

Repeat Refrain

Sometimes I thought it wasn't so bad.

Heroes

Words by David Bowie
Music by David Bowie and Brian Eno

recorded by David Bowie

I, I will be king.
And you, you will be queen.
Though nothing will drive them away,
We can beat them just for one day.
We can be heroes just for one day.

And you, you can be mean.
And I, I'll drink all the time.
'Cause we're lovers, and that is a fact.
Yes, we're lovers, and that is that.

Though nothing will keep us together,
We could steal time just for one day.
We can be heroes forever and ever.
What d'you say?

I wish you could swim
Like the dolphins, like dolphins can swim.
Though nothing, nothing will keep
    us together,
We can beat them forever and ever.
Oh, we can be heroes, just for one day.

I, I will be king.
And you, you will be queen.
Though nothing will drive them away,
We can be heroes just for one day.
We can be us just for one day.

I, I can remember
Standing by the wall.
The guns shot above our heads,
And we kissed as though nothing could fall.
And the shame was on the other side.
Oh, we can beat them forever and ever.
Then we could be heroes just for one day.
What d'you say?

We can be heroes.
We can be heroes.
We can be heroes just for one day.
We can be heroes.
We're nothing, and nothing will help us.
Maybe we're lying; then you better not stay.
But we could be safer just for one day.

Hey Joe

Words and Music by Billy Roberts

recorded by Jimi Hendrix

Hey Joe, where you goin' with that gun in your hand?
Hey Joe, I said, where you goin' with that gun in your hand?
Alright. I'm goin' down to shoot my old lady,
You know I caught her messin' 'round with another man. Yeah!
I'm goin' down to shoot my old lady,
You know I caught her messin' 'round with another man.
Huh! And that ain't too cool.

Hey Joe, I heard you shot your woman down, you shot her down now.
Hey Joe, I heard you shot you old lady down, you shot her down in the ground. Yeah!
Yes, I did, I shot her,
You know I caught her messin' 'round, messin' 'round town.
Yes I did, I shot her,
You know I caught my old lady messin' 'round town.
And I gave her the gun, I shot her!

Ah! Hey Joe! Alright!
Shoot her one more time again, baby! Ooh.
Hey Joe! Yeah! Ah, dig it!
Hey Joe! Ah! Joe, ah! Where you gonna go?
Ooh, alright.

Hey Joe, said now, where you gonna run to now, where you gonna run to? Yeah.
Hey Joe, I said, where you goin' to run to now, where you, where you gonna go?
Well, dig it! I'm goin' way down south, way down to Mexico way! Alright!
I'm goin' way down south, way down where I can be free.
Ain't no one gonna find me babe!

Ain't no hangman gonna, he ain't gonna put a rope around me!
You better believe it right now! I gotta go now!
Hey, hey, hey Joe, you better run on down!
Good-bye ev'rybody. Ow!
Hey, hey Joe, what'd I say, run on down.

Hit Me with Your Best Shot

Words and Music by Eddie Schwartz

recorded by Pat Benatar

Well, you're a real tough cookie
With a long history
Of breaking little hearts
Like the one in me.
That's O.K.
Let's see how you do it.
Put up your dukes.
Let's get down to it.

Refrain:
Hit me with your best shot.
Why don't you
Hit me with your best shot?
Hit me with your best shot.
Fire away.

You come on with a come on.
You don't fight fair.
But that's O.K.
See if I care.
Knock me down.
It's all in vain.
I'll get right back on
My feet again.

Refrain

Well, you're a real tough cookie
With a long history
Of breaking little hearts
Like the one in me.
Before I put another notch
In my lipstick case,
You better make sure
You put me in my place.

Refrain

Hot Blooded

Words and Music by Mick Jones and Lou Gramm

recorded by Foreigner

Well, I'm hot blooded, check it and see.
I got a fever of a hundred and three.
Come on baby, do you do more than dance?
I'm hot blooded, I'm hot blooded.

You don't have to read my mind to know
  what I have in mind.
Honey, you ought to know.
Now you move so fine, let me lay it on
  the line.
I wanna know what you're doin' after
  the show.
Now it's up to you. We can make a secret
  rendezvous.
Just me and you, I'll show you lovin' like you
  never knew.

That's why I'm hot blooded, check it
  and see.
I got a fever of a hundred and three.
Come on baby, do you do more than dance?
I'm hot blooded, hot blooded.

If it feels all right, maybe you can stay
  all night.
Should I leave you my key?
But you've got to give me a sign. Come on,
  girl, some kind of sign.
Tell me, are you hot, mama? You sure look
  that way to me.
Are you old enough? Will you be ready when
  I call your bluff?
Is my timing right? Did you save your love for
  me tonight?

Yeah, I'm hot blooded, check it and see.
I feel a fever burnin' inside of me.
Come on, baby, do you do more than dance?
I'm hot blooded, I'm hot blooded. I'm hot.

Now it's up to you. Can we make a secret
  rendezvous?
Oh, before we do, you'll have to get away
  from you know who.

Well, I'm hot blooded, check it and see.
I got a fever of a hundred and three.
Come on baby, do you do more than dance?
I'm hot blooded, I'm hot blooded.

(Hot blooded) Every night.
(Hot blooded) You're looking so tight.
(Hot blooded) Now you're driving me wild.
(Hot blooded) I'm so hot for you, child.
(Hot blooded) I'm a little bit high.
(Hot blooded) You're a little bit shy.
(Hot blooded) You're making me sing
(Hot blooded) For your sweet, sweet thing.
Did you hear what I say?

Hurts So Good

Words and Music by John Mellencamp and George Green

recorded by John Cougar Mellencamp

When I was a young boy,
Said, put away those young boy ways.
Now that I'm gettin' older, so much older,
I love all those young boy days.
With a girl like you, with a girl like you,
Lord knows there are things we can do, baby, just me and you.
Come on and make it

Refrain:
Hurt so good.
Come on, baby, make it hurt so good.
Sometimes love don't feel like it should.
You make it hurt so good.

Don't have to be so exciting.
Just try'n' to give myself a little bit of fun, yeah.
You always look so inviting.
You ain't as green as you are young.
Hey, baby, it's you. Come on, girl, now, it's you.
Sink your teeth right through my bones, baby.
Let's see what we can do.
Come on and make it

Refrain

I ain't talkin' no big deals;
I ain't made no plans myself.
I ain't talkin' no high heels.
Maybe we could walk around all day long,
Walk around all day long.

Refrain Twice

Hush

Words and Music by Joe South

recorded by Deep Purple

(Na, na na na, na na na, na na na.
Na, na na na, na na na, na na na.)

I got a certain little girl, she's on my mind.
No doubt about it, she looks so fine.
She's the best girl that I ever had.
Some time she's gonna make me feel so bad.

(Na, na na na, na na na, na na na.
Na, na na na, na na na, na na na.)

Refrain:
Hush, hush. I thought I heard her callin' my
    name, now.
Hush, hush. She broke my heart, but I love
    her just the same, now.
Hush, hush. I thought I heard her callin' my
    name, now.
Hush, hush. I need her lovin', and I'm not to
    blame, now.

(Love, love) We got it early in the morning.
(Love, love) We got it late in the evening.
(Love, love) Uh well, I want and need it.
(Love, love) Oh, I gotta gotta have it.

She's got lovin' like quicksand.
Only took one touch of her hand
To blow my mind, and I'm in so deep
That I can't eat, y'all, and I can't sleep.

(Na, na na na, na na na, na na na.
Na, na na na, na na na, na na na.)

Refrain

(Love, love) We got it early in the morning.
(Love, love) We got it late in the evening.
(Love, love) Oh, I gotta gotta have it.
(Na, na na na, na na na, na na na.
Na, na na na, na na na, na na na.
Na, na na na, na na na, na na na.)

I Can See for Miles

Words and Music by Peter Townshend

recorded by The Who

I know you've deceived me,
Here's a surprise.
I know that you have,
'Cause there's magic in my eyes.
I can see for miles and miles and miles
And miles and miles. Oh, yeah.

If you think that I don't know
About the little tricks you play,
And never see you
When deliberately you put things in my way.
Well, here's a poke at you.
You're gonna choke on it too.
You're gonna lose that smile.

Refrain:
Because all the while,
I can see for miles and miles.
I can see for miles and miles.
I can see for miles and miles and miles
And miles and miles. Oh, yeah.

You took advantage of my trust in you
When I was so far away.
I saw you holdin' lots of other guys,
And now you've got the nerve to say
That you still want me.
Well, that's as may be, but you gotta
    stand trial.

Refrain

Repeat Verse 1

Refrain

The Eiffel Tower and the Taj Mahal
Are mine to see on clear days.
You thought I would need a crystal ball
To see right through the haze.

Well, here's a poke at you.
You're gonna choke on it too.
You're gonna lose that smile.

Repeat Refrain and Fade

I Feel Fine

Words and Music by John Lennon and Paul McCartney

recorded by The Beatles

Baby's good to me you know,
She's happy as can be you know,
She said so.
I'm in love with her and I feel fine.

Baby says she's mine you know,
She tells me all the time you know,
She said so.
I'm in love with her and I feel fine.

I'm so glad she's telling all the world,
That her baby buys her things you know.
He buys her diamond rings you know,
She said so.
She's in love with me and I feel fine.

Baby says she's mine you know,
She tells me all the time you know,
She said so.
I'm in love with her and I feel fine.

I'm so glad that she's my little girl.
She's so glad she's telling all the world
That her baby buys her things you know,
He buys her diamond rings you know,
She said so.
She's in love with me and I feel fine.

I Fought the Law

Words and Music by Sonny Curtis

recorded by Bobby Fuller Four

A-breakin' rocks in the hot sun.
I fought the law and the law won.
I fought the law and the law won.
I needed money 'cause I had none.
I fought the law and the law won.
I fought the law and the law won.

I left my baby and I feel so bad.
I guess my race is run.
Well, she's the best girl I've ever had.
I fought the law and the law won.
I fought the law and the law won.

A-robbin' people with a six-gun.
I fought the law and the law won.
I fought the law and the law won.
I miss my baby and the good fun.
I fought the law and the law won.
I fought the law and the law won.

I left my baby and I feel so bad.
I guess my race is run.
Well, she's the best girl I've ever had.
I fought the law and the law won.
I fought the law and the law won.

I Shot the Sheriff

Words and Music by Bob Marley

recorded by Eric Clapton

I shot the sheriff, but I did not shoot
  the deputy.
I shot the sheriff, but I didn't shoot
  the deputy.

All around in my hometown,
They're trying to track me down.
They say they want to bring me in guilty
For the killing of a deputy,
For the life of a deputy.
But I say:

I shot the sheriff, but I swear it was in
  self-defense.
I shot the sheriff, and they say it is a capital
  offense.

Sheriff John Brown always hated me;
For what, I don't know.
And ev'ry time that I plant a seed,
He said, "Kill it before it grows."
He said, "Kill it before it grows."
But I say:

I shot the sheriff, but I swear it was in
  self-defense.
I shot the sheriff, but I swear it was in
  self-defense.

Freedom came my way one day,
And I started out of town.
All of a sudden I see sheriff John Brown
Aiming to shoot me down.
So I shot, I shot him down.
But I say:

I shot the sheriff, but I did not shoot
  the deputy.
I shot the sheriff, but I didn't shoot
  the deputy.

Reflexes get the better of me
And what is to be must be.
Ev'ry day the bucket goes to the well,
But one day the bottom will drop out.
Yes, one day the bottom will drop out.
But I say:

I shot the sheriff, but I didn't shoot
  the deputy.
I shot the sheriff, but I did not shoot
  no deputy.

I Won't Back Down

Words and Music by Jeff Lynne and Tom Petty

recorded by Tom Petty

Well, I won't back down.
No, I won't back down.
You can stand me up at the gates of hell,
But I won't back down.

Gonna stand my ground,
Won't be turned around.
And I'll keep this world from draggin' me around.
Stand my ground.
And I won't back down.

Hey, baby, there ain't no easy way out.
Hey, I will stand my ground,
And I won't back down.

Well, I know what's right.
I got just one life
In a world that keeps on pushin' me around,
But I'll stand my ground.
And I won't back down.

Hey, baby, there ain't no easy way out.
Hey, I will stand my ground.
Hey, baby, there ain't no easy way out.
Hey, I will stand my ground,
And I won't back down.
No, I won't back down.

Instant Karma

Words and Music by John Lennon

recorded by John Lennon

Instant karma's gonna get you,
Gonna knock you right on the head.
You better get yourself together.
Pretty soon you're gonna be dead.
What in the world you thinking of?
Laughing in the face of love?
What on earth you tryin' to do?
It's up to you, yeah, you.

Instant karma's gonna get you,
Gonna look you right in the face.
You better get yourself together, darlin'.
Join the human race.
How in the world you gonna see?
Laughin' at fools like me?
Who on earth d'you think you are?
A superstar?
Well, alright, you are.

Refrain:
Well, we all shine on,
Like the moon and the stars and the sun.
Well, we all shine on.
Everyone, come on.

Instant karma's gonna get you,
Gonna knock you off your feet.
Better recognize your brothers,
Everyone you meet.
Why in the world are we here?
Surely not to live in pain and fear.
Why on earth are you there
When you're everywhere?
Come and get your share.

Refrain Three Times

Repeat and Fade:
Well, we all shine on,
Like the moon and the stars and the sun.

Invisible Touch

Words and Music by Tony Banks, Phil Collins and Mike Rutherford

recorded by Genesis

Well, I've been waiting, waiting here so long,
But thinking nothing, nothing could go wrong.
But now I know she has a built-in ability
To take ev'rything she sees.
And now it seems I'm falling, falling for her.

Refrain:
She seems to have an invisible touch, yeah.
She reaches in and grabs right hold of your heart.
She seems to have an invisible touch, yeah.
It takes control and slowly tears you apart.

I don't really know her; I only know her name.
But she crawls under your skin, you're never quite the same.
And now I know she's got something you just can't trust,
Something mysterious.
And now it seems I'm falling, falling for her.

Refrain

She don't like losing; to her it's still a game.
And though she will mess up your life, you'll want her just the same,
And now I know she has a built-in ability
To take ev'rything she sees.
And now it seems I've fallen, fallen for her.

Refrain

It's a Heartache

Words and Music by Ronnie Scott and Steve Wolfe

recorded by Bonnie Tyler

It's a heartache,
Nothin' but a heartache,
Hits you when it's too late,
Hits you when you're down.
It's a fool's game,
Nothin' but a fool's game,
Standing in the cold rain,
Feeling like a clown.

It's a heartache,
Nothin' but a heartache,
Love him till your arms break,
Then he'll let you down.

It ain't right with love to share
When you find he doesn't care for you.
It ain't wise to need someone
As much as I depended on you.

Repeat Verse 1

It ain't right with love to share
When you find he doesn't care for you.
It ain't wise to need someone
As much as I depended on you.

It's a heartache,
Nothin' but a heartache,
You love him till your arms break,
Then he'll let you down.
It's a fool's game,
Nothin' but a fool's game,
Standing in the cold rain,
Feeling like a clown.

It's Only Love

Words and Music by Bryan Adams and Jim Vallance

recorded by Bryan Adams

When the feelin' is ended,
There ain't no use pretendin'.
Don't ya worry, well, it's only love.
When your world has been shattered,
Ain't nothin' else matters.
It ain't over, well, it's only love and that's all, yeah.

If your heart has been broken,
Hard words have been spoken,
It ain't easy, but it's only love.
And if your life ain't worth livin'
And you're ready to give in,
Just remember that it's only love.

You can live without the aggravation.
Ya gotta wanna win, ya gotta wanna win.
You keep lookin' back in desperation
Over and over and over again.

When your world is shattered,
Ain't nothin' else matters.
Well, it ain't over, it's only love.
If your life ain't worth livin'
And you're ready to give in,
Just remember that it's only love, yeah, that's all.

Yeah, it ain't easy, baby.
It's only love and that's all.

It's Only Rock 'n' Roll (But I Like It)

Words and Music by Mick Jagger and Keith Richards

recorded by The Rolling Stones

If I could stick my pen in my heart
I would spill it all over the stage.
Would it satisfy ya, would it slide on by ya,
Would you think the boy is strange? Ain't he strange?
If I could win ya, if I could sing ya
A love song so divine,
Would it be enough for your cheating heart
If I broke down and cried? If I cried?

Refrain:
I said I know it's only rock 'n' roll, but I like it.
I know it's only rock 'n' roll, but I like it, like it, yes, I do.
Oh, well, I like it, I like it, I like it.
I said, can't you see that this old boy has been-a lonely?

If I could stick a knife in my heart,
Suicide right on stage,
Would it be enough for your teenage lust,
Would it help to ease the pain? Ease your brain?
If I could dig down deep in my heart,
Feelings would flood on the page.
Would it satisfy ya, would it slide on by ya,
Would ya think the boy's insane? He's insane.

Refrain

And do ya think that you're the only girl around?
I bet you think that you're the only woman in town.

I said I know it's only rock 'n' roll, but I like it.
I know it's only rock 'n' roll, but I like it.
I know it's only rock 'n' roll, but I like it.
I know it's only rock 'n roll, but I like it, like it, yes, I do.
Oh, well, I like it, I like it.
I like it, I like it.

It's Still Rock and Roll to Me

Words and Music by Billy Joel

recorded by Billy Joel

What's the matter with the clothes I'm
  wearing?
"Can't you tell that your tie's too wide?"
Maybe I should buy some old tab collars?
"Welcome back to the age of jive.
Where have you been hidin' out lately honey?
You can't dress trashy till you spend a lot of
  money."
Everybody's talkin' 'bout the new sound.
Funny, but it's still rock and roll to me.

What's the matter with the car I'm driving?
"Can't you tell that it's out of style?"
Should I get a set of white wall tires?
"Are you gonna cruise the miracle mile?
Now a-days you can't be too sentimental.
Your best bet's a true baby blue Continental."
Hot funk, cool punk, even if it's old junk,
It's still rock and roll to me.

Oh, it doesn't matter what they say in the
  papers
'Cause it's always been the same old scene.
There's a new band in town
But you can't get the sound
From the story in a magazine
Aimed at your average teen.

How about a pair of pink side-wingers
And a bright orange pair of pants?
"Well you could really be a Beau Brummel,
Baby, if you just give it half a chance.

Don't waste your time on a new set of
  speakers.
You get more mileage from a cheap pair of
  sneakers."
Next phase, new wave dance craze, anyways,
It's still rock and roll to me.

Oh, it doesn't matter what they say in
  the papers
'Cause it's always been the same old scene.
There's a new band in town
But you can't get the sound
From the story in a magazine
Aimed at your average teen.

What's the matter with the crowd I'm seeing?
"Don't you know that they're out of touch?"
Should I try to be a straight A student?
"If you are, then you think too much."
"Don't you know about the new
  fashion honey?
All you need are looks and whole lot
  of money."
It's the next phase, new wave dance craze,
  anyways,
It's still rock and roll to me.

Everybody's talkin' 'bout the new sound.
Funny, but it's still rock and roll to me.

THE LYRIC LIBRARY

King of Pain

Written and Composed by Sting

recorded by The Police

There's a little black spot on the sun today
It's the same old thing as yesterday
There's a black hat caught in the high
tree-top
There's a flag-pole rag and the wind
won't stop
I have stood here before inside the
pouring rain
With the world turning circles running
'round my brain.
I guess I'm always hoping that you'll end
this reign
But it's my destiny to be the King of Pain.

There's a little black spot on the sun today;
That's my soul up there.
It's the same old thing as yesterday;
That's my soul up there.
There's a black hat caught in a high tree-top;
That's my soul up there.
There's a flag pole rag and the wind
won't stop;
That's my soul up there.

Refrain:
I have stood here before inside the
pouring rain
With the world turning circles
running 'round my brain.
I guess I'm always hoping that you'll end
this reign
But it's my destiny to be the King of Pain.

There's a fossil that's trapped in a high
cliff wall;
That's my soul up there.
There's a dead salmon frozen in a waterfall;
That's my soul up there.
There's a blue whale beached by a spring
tide's ebb;
That's my soul up there.
There's a butterfly trapped in a spider's web;
That's my soul up there.

Refrain

There's a king on a throne with his eyes
torn out,
There's a blind man looking for a shadow
of doubt;
There's a rich man sleeping on a bed,
There's a skeleton choking on a crust
of bread.

There's a red fox torn by a huntsman's pack;
That's my soul up there.
There's a little black spot on the sun today;
It's the same old thing as yesterday.

Refrain

Lady Madonna

Words and Music by John Lennon and Paul McCartney

recorded by The Beatles

Lady Madonna, children at your feet,
Wonder how you manage to make ends meet.
Who finds the money when you pay the rent?
Did you think that money was heaven sent?

Friday night arrives without a suitcase.
Sunday morning creeping like a nun.
Monday's child has learned to tie his bootlace.
See how they run.

Lady Madonna, baby at your breast,
Wonder how you manage to feed the rest.

See how they run.

Lady Madonna, lying on the bed,
Listen to the music playing in your head.

Tuesday afternoon is never ending,
Wednesday morning papers didn't come,
Thursday night your stockings needed mending,
See how they run.

Lady Madonna, children at your feet,
Wonder how you manage to make ends meet.

Land of Confusion

Words and Music by Tony Banks, Phil Collins and Mike Rutherford

recorded by Genesis

I must have dreamed a thousand dreams,
Been haunted by a million screams.
But I can hear the marching feet,
They're moving into the street.

Now did you read the news today?
They say the danger's gone away.
But I can see the fires still alight.
They're burning into the night.
There's too many men, too many people
Making too many problems,
And not much love to go around.
Can't you see this is a land of confusion?

Refrain:
Well, this is the world we live in,
And these are the hands we're given.
Use them and let's start trying
To make it a place worth living in.

Superman, where are you now?
Well, ev'rything's gone wrong somehow.
The men of steel, men of power,
They're losing control by the hour.
This is the time, this is the place.
So we look for the future,
But there's not much love to go around.
Tell me why this is a land of confusion.

Refrain

I remember long ago, when the sun
   was shining.
The shine, the stars were bright all through
   the night.
And the sound of your laughter as I held
   you tight.
So long ago.

I won't be coming home tonight.
My generation will put it right.
We're not just making promises
That we know we'll never keep.
There's too many men, too many people
Making too many problems,
And not much love to go around.
Can't you see this is a land of confusion?

Well, this is the world we live in,
And these are the hands we're given.
Use them and let's start trying
To make it a place worth fighting for.

This is the world we live in,
And these are the names we're given.
Stand up and let's start showing
Just where our lives are goin' to.

Landslide

Words and Music by Stevie Nicks

recorded by Fleetwood Mac

I took my love and I took it down.
I climbed a mountain and I turned around.
And I saw my reflection in the snow-covered hills
Till the landslide brought me down.

Oh, mirror in the sky, what is love?
Can the child within my heart rise above?
Can I sail through the changing ocean tides?
Can I handle the seasons of my life?
I don't know.

Refrain:
Well, I've been afraid of changing
'Cause I built my life around you.
But time makes you bolder. Children get older
And I'm getting older too.

Repeat Refrain

I'm getting older too.

So take this love, take it down.
Oh, if you climb a mountain and you turn around,
If you see my reflection in the snow-covered hills,
Well, the landslide will bring it down, down.
And if you see my reflection in the snow-covered hills,
Well, maybe the landslide'll bring it down.
Well, well, the landslide'll bring it down.

Last Child

Words and Music by Steven Tyler and Brad Whitford

recorded by Aerosmith

I'm dreaming tonight, I'm leaving back home.

Take me back to South Tallahassee,
Down 'cross the bridge to my sweet sassafrassy.
Can't stand up on my feet in the city,
Got to get back to the real nitty gritty.
Yes sir, no sir, don't come any closer to my
Home sweet home,
Can't catch no dose from a hot tail poontang sweetheart
Sweathog ready to make a silk purse from a
J. Paul Get and his ear
With a face in a beer.
Home sweet home.

Get out on the field, put the mule in the stable,
Ma, she's a-cookin' put the eats on the table.
Hate's in the city and my love's in the meadow,
Hand's on the plough and my feet's in the ghetto.
Stand up, sit down, don't do nothin',
It ain't no good when boss man's
Stuffin' it down their throats for paper notes
And their babies cry while cities lie at their feet
When you're rockin' in the streets.
Home sweet home.
Mama, take me home sweet home.

Repeat and Fade:
I was the last child, just a punk in the streets.

Lay Down Sally

Words and Music by Eric Clapton, Marcy Levy and George Terry

recorded by Eric Clapton

There is nothing that is wrong
In wanting you to stay here with me.
I know you've got somewhere to go,
But won't you make yourself at home and stay with me?
And don't you ever leave.

Refrain:
Lay down, Sally, and rest you in my arms.
Don't you think you want someone to talk to?
Lay down, Sally; no need to leave so soon.
I've been trying all night long just to talk to you.

The sun ain't nearly on the rise,
And we still got the moon and stars above.
Underneath the velvet skies,
Love is all that matters. Won't you stay with me?
And don't you ever leave.

Refrain

I long to see the morning light
Coloring your face so dreamily.
So don't you go and say good-bye;
You can lay your worries down and stay with me.
And don't you ever leave.

Refrain

Lay It on the Line

Words and Music by Mike Levine, Gil Moore, Rik Emmett and Ralph Santer

recorded by Triumph

It's the same old story all over again.
You turn a lover into just another friend.
I wanna love you. I wanna make you mine.
Won't you lay it on the line?

I'm tired of playing foolish games.
I'm tired of all of your lies making me insane.
Well, I don't ask for much, the truth will do just fine.
Won't you lay it on the line?

Refrain:
Lay it on the line.
Lay it on the line.
Lay it on the line.
Don't waste my time.

You've got no right to make me wait.
Better talk, girl, before it gets too late.
I never ever thought you could be so unkind.
Won't you lay it on the line?

Refrain

You know I love you, you know it's true.
It's up to you, girl, now what've I got to do?
Don't hold me up, girl, don't waste my precious time.
Won't you lay it on the line?

Four Times:
Lay it on the line.
Lay it on the line.

Layla

Words and Music by Eric Clapton and Jim Gordon

recorded by Derek & The Dominos

What will you do when you get lonely
With nobody waiting by your side?
You've been running and hiding much too long.
You know it's just your foolish pride.

Refrain:
Layla, you got me on my knees, Layla,
I'm begging darling please, Layla,
Darling won't you ease my worried mind.

Tried to give you consolation,
Your old man won't let you down.
Like a fool I fell in love with you,
Turned the whole world upside down.

Refrain

Let's make the best of the situation
Before I finally go insane.
Please don't say we'll never find a way
And tell me all my love's in vain.

Refrain

Repeat and Fade:
Layla, you've got me on my knees, Layla,
I'm begging darling, please…

Learning to Fly

Words and Music by Jeff Lynne and Tom Petty

recorded by Tom Petty

Well, I started out down a dirty road,
Started out all alone.
And the sun went down as I crossed the hill,
And the town lit up, the world got still.
I'm learning to fly, but I ain't got wings.
Coming down is the hardest thing.

Well, the good ol' days may not return,
And the rocks might melt and the sea may burn.
I'm learning to fly around the clouds.
What goes up must come down.

Well, some say life will beat you down
And break your heart, steal your crown.
So I started out for God knows where.
I guess I'll know when I get there.
I'm learning to fly, but I ain't got wings.
Coming down is the hardest thing.

I'm learning to fly around the clouds.
What goes up must come down.
I'm learning to fly.
I'm learning to fly.

Leave It

Words and Music by Trevor Horn, Trevor Rabin and Chris Squire

recorded by Yes

I can feel no sense of measure,
No illusions as we take
Refuge in young man's pleasure,
Breaking down the dreams we make real.

One down, one to go;
Another town and one more show.
Downtown they're giving away,
But she never came back.
No phone can take your place;
You know what I mean.
We have the same intrigue
As a court of kings.

Ah, leave it.
Ah, leave it.

Two down, there you go.
MacArthur Park in the driving snow.
Uptown they're digging out;
Better lay your claim.
Get home; you're not alone.
You just broke out of the danger zone.
Be there to show your face
On another dreamy day.

Refrain:
Ah, leave it.
(Good-bye, good-bye, good-bye bad.
Hello, hello, heaven.)
Ah, leave it.
(Good-bye, good-bye, good-bye bad.
Hello, hello, heaven.)

Repeat Verse 1

Refrain

Twice:
One down, one to go;
Another town and one more show.
(Good-bye, good-bye, good-bye bad.
Hello, hello, heaven.)

Leave it.

Legend of a Mind

Words and Music by Ray Thomas

recorded by The Moody Blues

Timothy Leary's dead.
No, no, he's outside looking in.
Timothy Leary's dead.
No, no, he's outside looking in.
He'll fly his astro plane,
Takes you trips around the bay,
Brings you back the same day,
Timothy Leary, Timothy Leary.

Repeat Verse 1

Along the coast you'll hear them boast
About a light they say that shines so clear.
So raise your glass, we'll drink a toast
To the little man who sells you thrills along the pier.

He'll take you up, he'll bring you down,
He'll plant your feet back firmly on the ground.
He flies so high, he swoops so low,
He knows exactly which way he's gonna go.
Timothy Leary, Timothy Leary.

He'll take you up, he'll bring you down,
He'll plant your feet back on the ground.
He'll fly so high, he'll swoop so low.
Timothy Leary.

He'll fly his astro plane.
He'll take you trips around the bay.
He'll bring you back the same day.
Timothy Leary, Timothy Leary,
Timothy Leary, Timothy Leary,
Timothy Leary.

Let It Rain

Words and Music by Eric Clapton and Bonnie Bramlett

recorded by Eric Clapton

The rain is falling
Through the mist of sorrow that surrounded me.
The sun could melt the fog away,
The mist that may surround me.

Refrain:
Let it rain; let it rain.
Let your love rain down on me.
Let it rain; let it rain.
Let it rain, rain, rain.

My life was like a desert flower,
Burning in the sun.
Until I found the way to love,
The heart was sad and done.

Refrain

Now I know the secret;
There is nothing that I lack.
If I give my love to you,
Be sure to give it back.

Refrain

Let It Ride

Words and Music by Randy Bachman and Charles Turner

recorded by Bachman-Turner Overdrive

Goodbye, hard life, don't cry. Would you let it ride?
Goodbye, hard life, don't cry. Would you let it ride?

You can't see the mornin',
But I can see the light.
Ride, ride, ride, let it ride.
While you've been out runnin'
I've been waiting half the night.
Ride, ride, ride, let it ride.

Refrain:
And would you cry if I told you that I lied,
And would you say goodbye or would you let it ride.

Babe, my life is not complete;
I never see you smile.
Ride, ride, ride, let it ride.
Baby you want the forgivin' kind
And that's just not my style.
Ride, ride, ride, let it ride.

Refrain

I've been doin' things worthwhile
And you've been bookin' time.

Refrain

Four Times:
Would you let it ride?

Five Times:
Ride, ride, ride, let it ride.

Four Times:
Would you let it ride?

The Logical Song

Words and Music by Rick Davies and Roger Hodgson

recorded by Supertramp

When I was young, it seemed that life was so wonderful,
A miracle, oh it was beautiful, magical.
And all the birds in the trees, well they'd sing so happily,
Joyfully, playfully watching me.

But then they sent me away to teach me how to be sensible,
Logical, responsible, practical.
And they showed me a world where I could be so dependable,
Clinical, intellectual, cynical.

There are times when all the world's asleep,
The questions run too deep for such a simple man.
Won't you please, please tell me what we've learned.
I know it sounds absurd, but please tell me who I am.

Now watch what you say or they'll be calling you a radical.
Liberal, fanatical, criminal.
Won't you sign up your name, we'd like to feel you're
Acceptable, respectable, presentable, a vegetable!

At night, when all the world's asleep,
The questions run so deep for such a simple man.
Won't you please tell me what we've learned.
I know it sounds absurd, but please tell me who I am.

Long Cool Woman (In a Black Dress)

Words and Music by Allan Clarke, Roger Cook and Roger Greenaway

recorded by The Hollies

Saturday night I was downtown
Working for the F.B.I.
Sitting in a nest of bad men,
Whiskey bottles piling high.
Bootlegging boozer on the west-side
Full of people who are doing wrong.
Just about to call up the D.A. man
When I heard this woman singing a song.

A pair of forty-fives made me open my eyes,
My temperature started to rise.
She was a long cool woman in a black dress.
Just a five-nine beautiful tall.
With just one look I was a bad mess
'Cause that long cool woman had it all.

I saw her head up to the table.
Well, a tall walking big black cat.
When Charlie said, "I hope that you're able."
Boy, I'm telling you she knows where it's at.
Suddenly we heard the sirens,
And everybody started to run.
Jumpin' out of doors and tables
When I heard somebody shooting a gun.

Well, the D.A. was pumping my left hand
And she was holding my right.
Well, I told her don't get scared
'Cause you're gonna be spared.
Well, I'm gonna be forgiven
'Cause I wanna spend my living
With a long cool woman in a black dress.
Just a five-nine beautiful tall.
With just one look I was a bad mess
'Cause that long cool woman had it all.
Had it all.
Had it all…

Love Hurts

Words and Music by Boudleaux Bryant

recorded by Nazareth

Love hurts, love scars, love wounds and mars
Any heart not tough nor strong enough
To take a lot of pain, take a lot of pain.
Love is like a cloud, holds a lot of rain.
Love hurts, love hurts.

I'm young, I know, but even so
I know a thing or two. I've learned from you;
I've really learned a lot, really learned a lot.
Love is like a stove, burns you when it's hot.
Love hurts, love hurts.

Some fools rave on happiness, blissfulness, togetherness.
Some fools fool themselves, I guess,
But they're not fooling me.
I know it isn't true, know it isn't true.
Love is just a lie made to make you blue.
Love hurts, love hurts.

Love Is a Battlefield

Words and Music by Mike Chapman and Holly Knight

recorded by Pat Benatar

Refrain:
We are young.
Heartache to heartache we stand;
No promises, no demands.
Love is a battlefield.
We are strong.
No one can tell us we're wrong,
Searching our hearts for so long,
Both of us knowing love is a battlefield.

You're begging me to go, then making me stay.
Why do you hurt me so bad?
It would help me to know, do I stand in your way,
Or am I the best thing you've had?
Believe me, believe me, I can't tell you why,
But I'm trapped by your love and I'm chained to your side.

Refrain

When I'm losing control, will you turn me away
Or touch me deep inside?
And when all this gets old, will it still feel the same?
There's no way this will die.
But if we get much closer I could lose control,
And if your heart surrenders, you'll need me to hold.

Refrain

Maggie May

Words and Music by Rod Stewart and Martin Quittenton

recorded by Rod Stewart

Wake up, Maggie,
I think I got something to say to you.
It's late September
And I really should be back at school.
I know I keep you amused,
But I feel I'm being used.
Oh, Maggie, I couldn't have tried any more.
You led me away from home
Just to save you from being alone.
You stole my heart,
And that's what really hurts.

The morning sun, when it's in your face,
Really shows your age.
But that don't worry me none.
In my eyes you're everything.
I laughed at all of your jokes.
My love you didn't need to coax.
Oh, Maggie, I couldn't have tried any more.
You led me away from home
Just to save you from being alone.
You stole my heart,
And that's a pain I can do without.

All I needed was a friend
To lend a guiding hand.
But you turned into a lover,
And, mother, what a lover!
You wore me out.
All you did was wreck my bed,
And, in the morning, kick me in the head.
Oh, Maggie, I couldn't have tried any more.
You led me away from home
'Cause you didn't want to be alone.
You stole my heart.
I couldn't leave you if I tried.

I suppose I could collect my books
And get on back to school.
Or steal my daddy's cue
And make a living out of playing pool.
Or find myself a rock 'n' roll band
That needs a helping hand.
Oh, Maggie, I wish I'd never seen your face.
You made a first-class fool out of me.
But I'm as blind as a fool can be.
You stole my heart,
But I love you anyway.

The Magic Bus

Words and Music by Peter Townshend

recorded by The Who

Every day I get in the queue (too much, the magic bus)
To get on the bus that takes me to you (too much, the magic bus).
I'm so nervous, I just sit and smile (too much, the magic bus).
You house is only another mile (too much, the magic bus).

Thank you, driver, for getting me here (let's drive the magic bus).
You'll be an inspector, have no fear (let's drive the magic bus).
I don't wish to cause a fuss (let's drive the magic bus).
Can I buy your magic bus? (let's drive the magic bus)

I don't care how much I pay (too much, the magic bus).
Wanna drive my bus to my baby each day (too much, the magic bus).
Ev'ry day you would see the dust (too much, the magic bus)
As I drove to my baby in my magic bus (too much, the magic bus).

Magic bus, I want it, I want it.
Magic bus, I want it, I want it.

Me and Bobby McGee

Words and Music by Kris Kristofferson and Fred Foster

recorded by Janis Joplin

Busted flat in Baton Rouge,
Waitin' for a train,
When I's feelin' near as faded as my jeans.
Bobby thumbed a diesel down
Just before it rained;
It rode us all the way in to New Orleans.

I pulled my harpoon out of my dirty red
    bandana.
I was playin' sad while Bobby sang the
    blues, yeah.
Windshield wipers slappin' time,
I's holdin' Bobby's hand in mine;
We sang ev'ry song that driver knew, yeah.

Freedom's just another word for nothin'
    left to lose.
Nothin', I mean nothin', hon' if it ain't
    free, no, no.
Yeah, feelin' good was easy, Lord,
When he sang the blues.
You know, feelin' good was good enough
    for me,
Good enough for me an' my Bobby McGee.

From the Kentucky coal mine
To the California sun,
Bobby shared the secrets of my soul;
Through all kinds of weather,
Through everything we done,
Yeah, Bobby baby kept me from the cold.

One day a-near Salinas, Lord,
I let him slip away.

He's lookin' for that home, I hope he finds it.
But I'd trade all of my tomorrows
For one single yesterday
To be holdin' Bobby's body next to mine.

Freedom's just another word for nothin'
    left to lose,
Nothin', and that's all that Bobby left me,
    yeah.
But if feelin' good was easy, Lord,
When he sang the blues;
Hey, feelin' good was good enough for me,
    mm hmm,
Good enough for me and my Bobby McGee.

La da da, *etc.*
La da da, *etc.*, Bobby McGee, hey.
La da la, *etc.*
La la la, *etc.*, Bobby McGee.
La da da, *etc.*
Hey now, Bobby, lo now, Bobby McGee, yeah.
Lo na lo, *etc.*
Hey now, Bobby, lo now, Bobby McGee, yeah.
And then when I called him my lover, called
    him my man;
I said I called my lover, did the best I can.
Come on, hey now, Bobby, now,
Hey now, Bobby McGee, yeah.
Lo la lo, *etc.*
Hey, hey, Bobby McGee, Lord.

La la la, *etc.*
Hey, hey, hey, Bobby McGee, ah.

Message in a Bottle

Written and Composed by Sting

recorded by The Police

Just a castaway,
An island lost at sea-o.
Anuzzer lonely day
No one here but me-o.
More loneliness than any man could bear.
Rescue me before I fall into despair-o.

Refrain:
I'll send an S.O.S. to the world.
I'll send an S.O.S. to the world.
I hope that someone gets my,
I hope that someone gets my,
I hope that someone gets my
Message in a bottle, yeah,
Message in a bottle, yeah.

A year has passed since I wrote my note,
But I should have known this right from the start.
Only hope can keep me together.
Love can mend your life, but love can break your heart.

Refrain

Walked out this morning,
I don't believe what I saw.
A hundred billion bottles washed up on the shore.
Seems like I'm not alone in being alone.
A hundred billion castaways looking for a home.

Refrain

I'm sending out an S.O.S.

Miss You

Words and Music by Mick Jagger and Keith Richards

recorded by The Rolling Stones

I've been holding out so long,
I've been sleeping all alone,
Lord I miss you.
I've been hanging on the phone,
I've been sleeping all alone,
I want to kiss you.

Hoo hoo hoo hoo...

Well, I've been haunted in my sleep,
You've been starring in my dreams,
Lord I miss you, child.
I've been waiting in the hall,
Been waiting on your call
When the phone rings.

Spoken:
It's just some friends of mine that say,
"Hey, what's the matter man?
We're gonna come around at twelve o'clock
With some Puerto Rican girls
That are just dyin' to meet you.
We're gonna bring a case of wine,
Hey, let's go mess and fool around,
You know we used to."

Sung:
Ha ha ha...

Everybody waits so long,
Oh! Baby, why you wait so long?
Won't you come on?
Come on!

Spoken:
I've been walking in Central Park,
Singing after dark,
People think I'm crazy.
I've been stumbling on my feet,
Shuffling thro' the street
Asking people,
"What's the matter with you, Jim boy?"
Sometimes what I want to say to myself,
Sometimes I say:

Sung:
Hoo hoo hoo hoo...

I guess I'm lying to myself,
It's just you and no one else,
Lord I won't miss you child.
You've just been blotting out my mind,
Fooling on my time,
No I won't miss you baby.
Lord I miss your touch.
Oh ooh.
Ha ha ha ha...

Mississippi Queen

Words and Music by Leslie West, Felix Pappalardi, Corky Laing and David Rea

recorded by Mountain

Mississippi Queen,
If you know what I mean
Mississippi Queen,
She taught me everything.

Way down around Bicksburg,
Around Louisiana way,
Lives a Cajun lady
Called the Mississippi Queen.

Refrain:
You know she was a dancer,
She moved better on wine.
While the rest of them dudes was gettin' their kicks,
Buddy, beg your pardon, I was gettin' mine.

Mississippi Queen,
If you know what I mean.
Mississippi Queen,
She taught me everything.

This lady, she asked me,
If I would be her man.
You know that I told her
I'd do what I can
To keep her lookin' pretty,
Buy her dresses that shine.
While the rest of them dudes was makin' their bread,
Buddy, beg your pardon, I was losin' mine.

Refrain

Hey, Mississippi Queen.

Money

Words and Music by Roger Waters

recorded by Pink Floyd

Money, ya get away.
Ya get a good job with more pay, and you're OK.
Money, it's a gas.
Grab that cash with both hands and make a stash.
New car, caviar, four-star daydream,
Think I'll buy me a football team.

Money, you get back.
I'm all right, Jack. Keep your hands off of my stack.
Money, it's a hit.
But don't give me that do-goody-good bullshit.
I'm in the high-fidelity, first-class trav'ling set,
And I think I need a Lear jet.

Money, it's a crime.
Share it fairly, but don't take a slice of my pie.
Money, so they say,
Is the root of all evil today.
But if you ask for a rise, it's no surprise
That they're giving none away.

Money for Nothing

Words and Music by Mark Knopfler and Sting

recorded by Dire Straits

I want my, I want my MTV.

Now, look at them yo-yos, that's the way
   you do it,
You play the guitar on the MTV.
That ain't workin', that's the way you do it,
Money for nothin' and your chicks for free.
Now, that ain't workin', that's the way you
   do it,
Lemme tell ya, them guys ain't dumb.
You maybe get a blister on your little finger,
Maybe get a blister on your thumb.

Refrain:
We gotta install microwave ovens,
Custom kitchen deliveries.
We gotta move these refrigerators,
We gotta move these color TVs.

That little faggot with the earring and
   the makeup,
Yeah, buddy, that's his own hair.
That little faggot got his own jet airplane.
That little faggot, he's a millionaire.

Refrain Twice

I shoulda learned to play the guitar,
I shoulda learned to play them drums.
Look at that mama, she got it. Stickin' in the
   camera, man,
We could have some.
And he's up there. What's that? Hawaiian
   noises?
He's bangin' on the bongos like a
   chimpanzee.
Oh, that ain't workin', that's the way you
   do it,
Get your money for nothin', get your chicks
   for free.

Refrain

Now, that ain't workin', that's the way
   you do it,
You play the guitar on the MTV.
That ain't workin', that's the way you do it,
Money for nothin' and your chicks for free.
Money for nothin', and chicks for free.
Get your money for nothin' and your chicks
   for free.

Repeat and Fade:
Get your money for nothin' and your chicks
   for free.
I want my, I want my, I want my MTV.

My Generation

Words and Music by Peter Townshend

recorded by The Who

People try to put us down (talkin' 'bout my generation)
Just because we get around (talkin' 'bout my generation).
Things they do look awful cold (talkin' 'bout my generation).
I hope I die before I get old (talkin' 'bout my generation).
This is my generation,
This is my generation, baby.

Why don't you all fade away (talkin' 'bout my generation).
Don't try to dig what we all say (talkin' 'bout my generation).
I'm not tryin' to cause a big sensation (talkin' 'bout my generation).
I'm just talkin' 'bout my generation (talkin' 'bout my generation).
This is my generation.
This is my generation, baby.

New Kid in Town

Words and Music by John David Souther, Don Henley and Glenn Frey

recorded by The Eagles

There's talk on the street; it sounds so
   familiar.
Great expectations, everybody's
   watching you.
People you meet, they all seem to know you.
Even your old friends treat you like you're
   something new.
Johnny-come-lately, the new kid in town.
Everybody loves you, so don't let them down.

You look in her eyes; the music begins
   to play.
Hopeless romantics, here we go again.
But after a while you're looking the
   other way.
It's those restless hearts that never mend.
Johnny-come-lately, the new kid in town.
Will she still love you when you're
   not around?

There's so many things you should have
   told her,
But night after night you're willing to
   hold her,
Just hold her.
Tears on your shoulder.

There's talk on the street; it's there to
   remind you
That it doesn't really matter which side
   you're on.

You're walking away and they're talking
   behind you.
They will never forget you till somebody new
   comes along.

Where you been lately?
There's a new kid in town.
Everybody loves him, don't they?
No he's holding her, and you're still around.
Oh, my, my.

There's a new kid in town,
Just another new kid in town.
Ooh, hoo.
Everybody's talking 'bout the new kid
   in town,
Ooh, hoo.
Everybody's walking like the new kid
   in town.
There's a new kid in town.
I don't want to hear it. There's a new kid
   in town.
I don't want to hear it. There's a new kid
   in town.

Nights in White Satin

Words and Music by Justin Hayward

recorded by The Moody Blues

Nights in white satin,
Never reaching the end,
Letters I've written,
Never meaning to send.

Beauty I've always missed
With these before,
Just what the truth is
I can't say anymore.

'Cause I love you.
Yes, I love you.
Oh, how I love you.

Gazing at people,
Some hand in hand,
Just what I'm going through,
They can't understand.

Some try to tell me
Thoughts they cannot defend,
Just what you want to be
You'll be in the end.

And I love you.
Yes, I love you.
Oh, how I love you.

One More Night

Words and Music by Phil Collins

recorded by Phil Collins

I've been trying for so long
To let you know,
Let you know how I feel,
And if I stumble, if I fall
Just help me back,
So I can make you see.

Please give me one more night,
Give me one more night.
One more night,
'Cause I can't wait forever.
Give me just one more night,
Oh, just one more night,
Oh, one more night,
'Cause I can't wait forever.

I've been sitting here so long
Wasting time,
Just staring at the phone,
And I was wondering should I call you
Then I thought,
Maybe you're not alone.

Please give me one more night,
Give me just one more night,
One more night.
'Cause I can't wait forever.
Please give me one more night,
Oh, just one more night,
Oh, one more night,
'Cause I can't wait forever.

Give me one more night,
Give me just one more night,
Just one more night
'Cause I can't wait forever.

Like a river to the sea,
I will always be with you,
And if you sail away
I will follow you.
Give me one more night,
Give me just one more night,
Oh, one more night
'Cause I can't wait forever.

I know there'll never be a time
You'll ever feel the same,
And I know it's only right.
But if you change your mind,
You know that I'll be here,
And maybe we both can learn.

Give me just one more night,
Give me just one more night.
One more night,
'Cause I can't wait forever.
Give me just one more night,
Give me just one more night,
Oh, one more night,
'Cause I can't wait forever.

Ooh, ooh, ooh...

One Thing Leads to Another

Words and Music by Cy Curnin, Jamie West-Oram, Adam Woods, Rupert Greenall and Alfred Agius

recorded by The Fixx

The deception with tact;
Just what are you trying to say?
You've got a blank face which irritates.
Communicate; pull out your party piece.
You see dimensions in two,
State your case in black or white.
But when one little cross leads to shots,
    grit your teeth,
You run for cover, so discreet.

Refrain:
Why don't they do what they say;
Say what you mean?
One thing leads to another.
You told me something wrong;
I know I listen too long, but then
One thing leads to another.

The impression that you sell
Passes in and out like a scent.
But the long face that you see
Comes from living close to your fears.
If this is up, then I'm up, but you're
    running out of sight.
You've seen your name on the walls.
And when one little bump leads to shock,
    miss a beat,
You run for cover and there's heat.

Refrain

Yeah, yeah, yeah.
One thing, one thing leads to another.

Then it's easy to believe
Somebody's been lying to me.
But when the wrong word goes in the
    right ear,
I know you've been lying to me.
It's getting rough; off the cuff
I've got to say enough's enough.
Bigger, the harder he falls.
But when the wrong antidote is like a
    bulge on the throat.
You run for cover in the heat.

Refrain

Yeah, yeah, yeah.
One thing, one thing leads to another.

Only the Good Die Young

Words and Music by Billy Joel

recorded by Billy Joel

Come out, Virginia, don't let me wait.
You Catholic girls start much too late,
Ah, but sooner or later it comes down
    to fate.
I might as well be the one.

Well they showed you a statue and told
    you to pray.
They built you a temple and locked you away,
Ah, but they never told the price that you pay,
The things that you might have done,

For only the good die young,
That's what I said.
Only the good die young,
Only the good die young.

You might have heard I run with a
    dangerous crowd.
We ain't too pretty, we ain't too proud.
We might be laughing a bit too loud,
But that never hurt no one.

So come on Virginia, show me a sign,
Send up a signal, I'll throw you a line.
That stained glass curtain you're
    hiding behind
Never lets in the sun.

Darlin', only the good die young, woah,
Only the good die young.
Only the good die young.

You got a nice white dress and a party on
    your confirmation.
You've got a brand new soul,
And a cross of gold.
It's a pity they didn't give you quite enough
    information.
You didn't count on me
When you were counting on your rosary.
Oh, oh, oh.

And they say there's a heaven for those
    who will wait.
Some say it's better, but I say it ain't.
I'd rather laugh with the sinners than cry
    with the saints;
The sinners are much more fun.

You know that only the good die young,
That's what I say.
Only the good die young,
Only the good die young.

Said your mother told you
All I could give was a reputation.
She never cared for me,
But did she ever say a prayer for me?

Repeat from Top and Fade

Over Under Sideways Down

Words and Music by Geoff Beck, Christopher Dreja, Keith Relf and James McCarty

recorded by The Yardbirds

(Hey! Hey! Hey! Hey!)
Cars and girls are easy come by in this day and age.
Laughing, joking, dreams, weed smoking, till I've spent my wage.
When I was young, people spoke of immorality.
All the things they said were wrong are what I want to be.

Refrain:
(Hey!) Over, under, sideways, down,
(Hey!) I bounce a ball that's square and round.
(Hey!) Over, under, sideways, down,
(Hey!) I bounce a ball that's square and round.
When will it end? (When will it end?)
When will it end? (When will it end?)

(Hey! Hey! Hey! Hey!)
I find comments 'bout my looks irrelativity.
Think I'll go and have some fun, 'cause it's all for free.
I'm not searchin' for a reason to enjoy myself.
Seems it's better done than argue with somebody else.

Refrain

Owner of a Lonely Heart

Words and Music by Trevor Horn, Jon Anderson, Trevor Rabin and Chris Squire

recorded by Yes

Move yourself.
You always live your life
Never thinking of the future.
Prove yourself.
You are the move you make.
Take your chances, win or loser.
See yourself.
You are the steps you take.
You and you, and that's the only way.
Shake, shake yourself.
You've ev'ry move you make.
So the story goes.

Refrain:
Owner of a lonely heart.
Owner of a lonely heart.
(Much better than a)
Owner of a broken heart.
Owner of a lonely heart.

Say you don't want to change it.
You've been hurt so before.
Watch it now,
The eagle in the sky,
How he dancin' one and only.
You lose yourself.
No, not for pity's sake.
There's no real reason to be lonely.
Be yourself.
Give your free will a chance.
You've got to want to succeed.

Refrain

After my own indecision,
They confused me so.
My love said never question your will at all.
In the end you've got to go.
Look before you leap
And don't you hesitate at all. No, no.

Refrain Twice

Sooner or later each conclusion
Will decide the lonely heart.
(Owner of a lonely heart.)
It will excite it,
Will delight it,
Will give a better start.
(Owner of a lonely heart.)
Don't deceive your free will at all.

Twice:
Don't deceive your free will at all.
Don't deceive your free will at all.
Just receive it.
Just receive it.

Paradise by the Dashboard Light

Words and Music by Jim Steinman

recorded by Meat Loaf

Boy:
I remember every little thing as if it happened only yesterday,
Parking by the lake, and there was not another car in sight.
And I never had a girl looking any better than you did,
And all the kids at school, they were wishing they were me that night.

Refrain 1:
And now our bodies are, oh, so close and tight.
It never felt so good, it never felt so right.
And we're glowing like the metal on the edge of a knife,
Glowing like the metal on the edge of a knife.
C'mon! Hold on tight! Well, c'mon! Hold on tight!
Though it's cold and lonely in the deep, dark night,
I can see paradise by the dashboard light.

Girl:
Ain't no doubt about it, we were doubly blessed,
'Cause we were barely seventeen and we were barely dressed.

Both:
Ain't no doubt about it. Baby, gotta go out and shout it.
Ain't no doubt about it, we were doubly blessed.

Boy:
'Cause we were barely seventeen and we were barely dressed.

Baby don'tcha hear my heart, you got it drowning out the radio.
I've been waiting so long for you to come along and have some fun.
And I gotta let ya know, no, you're never gonna regret it.
So open up your eyes, I got a big surprise,
It'll feel all right, well, I wanna make your motor run.

Refrain 1

Though it's cold and lonely in the deep, dark night,
I can see paradise by the dashboard light.

You got to do what you can, and let Mother Nature do the rest.
Ain't no doubt about it, we were doubly blessed,
'Cause we were barely seventeen and we were barely...

We're gonna go all the way tonight,
We're gonna go all the way and tonight's the night.
We're gonna go all the way tonight,
We're gonna go all the way and tonight's the night.

Baseball Play-by-Play on the Car Radio:
OK, here we go, we got a real pressure cooker going here, two down, nobody on, no score, bottom of the ninth, there's the wind-up, and there it is, a line shot up the middle, look at him go. This boy can really fly!

He's rounding first and really turning it on now, he's not letting up at all, he's gonna try for second; the ball is bobbled out in center, and here's the throw, and what a throw! He's gonna slide in head first, here he comes, he's out! No, wait, safe, safe at second base, this kid really makes things happen out there.

Batter steps up to the plate, here's the pitch—he's going, and what a jump he's got, he's trying for third, here's the throw, it's in the dirt—safe at third! Holy cow, stolen base!

He's taking a pretty big lead out there, almost daring them to try and pick him off. The pitcher glances over, winds up, and it's bunted, bunted down the third base line, the suicide squeeze is on! Here he comes, squeeze play, it's gonna be close, here's the throw, here's the play at the plate, holy cow, I think he's gonna make it!

Girl:
Stop right there!
I gotta know right now, before we go any further,

(continues)

("Paradise by the Dashboard Light," *continued*)

Twice:
Do you love me? Will you love me forever?
Do you need me? Will you never leave me?
Will you make me so happy for the rest of my life?
Will you take me away, and will you make me your wife?
I gotta know right now, before we go any further,
Do you love me? Will you love me forever?

Boy (Refrain 2, Repeat Three Times):
Let me sleep on it. Baby, baby, let me sleep on it.
Let me sleep on it, and I'll give you an answer in the morning.

Girl (Refrain 3):
I gotta know right now!
Do you love me? Will you love me forever?
Do you need me? Will you never leave me?
Will you make me so happy for the rest of my life?
Will you take me away, and will you make me your wife?
I gotta know right now before we go any further,
Do you love me? Will you love me forever?

Spoken:
What's it gonna be, boy? Come on! I can wait all night.
What's it gonna be, boy, yes or no?
What's it gonna be, boy, yes or no?

Boy: Refrain 2

Girl: Refrain 3

Boy:
Let me sleep on it.

Girl:
Will you love me forever?

Boy:
Let me sleep on it.

Girl:
Will you love me forever?
Boy:
I couldn't take it any longer, Lord, I was crazed,
And when the feeling came upon me like a tidal wave,
I started swearing to my God and on my mother's grave
That I would love you to the end of time,
I swore that I would love you to the end of time!
So now I'm praying for the end of time to hurry up and arrive,
'Cause if I gotta spend another minute with you,
I don't think that I can really survive.
I'll never break my promise or forget my vow,
But God only knows what I can do right now.
I'm praying for the end of time, it's all that I can do.
Praying for the end of time, so I can end my time with you.

Boy:
Well, it was long ago, and it was far away,
And it was so much better than it is today.

Girl:
It never felt so good, it never felt so right,

Philadelphia Freedom

Words and Music by Elton John and Bernie Taupin

recorded by Elton John

I used to be a rolling stone, you know
If the cause was right.
I'd leave
To find the answer on the road.
I used to be a heart beating for someone.
But the times have changed,
The less I say the more my work gets done.

Refrain:
'Cause I live and breathe this Philadelphia
    freedom.
From the day that I was born I waved the
    flag.
Philadelphia freedom took me knee-high to
    a man, yeah!
Gave me peace of mind my daddy never had.
Oh, Philadelphia freedom
Shine on me,
I love it.
Shine the light
Through the eyes of the one left behind.
Shine the light, shine the light.
Shine the light. Won't you shine the light?
Philadelphia freedom,
I love-ove-ove you,
Yes I do.

If you choose to, you can live your life alone.
Some people choose the city,
Some others choose the good old family
    home.
I like living easy without family ties,
'Til the whippoorwill of freedom zapped me
Right between the eyes.

Refrain

Oh, Philadelphia freedom
Shine on me,
I love it.
Shine the light
Through the eyes of the one left behind.
Shine the light, shine the light.
Shine the light. Won't you shine the light?
Philadelphia freedom,
I love-ove-ove you,
Don't you know I love you?
Don't you know I love you?
Yes I do.
(Philadelphia freedom)
I love-ove-ove you, yes I do.

Repeat and Fade:
(Philadelphia freedom)
Don't you know that I love -ove-ove you,
Yes I do.

Piece of My Heart

Words and Music by Bert Berns and Jerry Ragovoy

recorded by Janis Joplin with Big Brother & The Holding Company

Didn't I make you feel
Like you were the only man?
Didn't I give you everything that a woman possibly can?
But with all the love I give you,
It's never enough,
But I'm gonna show you, baby,
That a woman can be tough.

Refrain:
So go on, go on, go on, go on,
Take it!
Take another piece of my heart now, baby.
Break it!
Break another little piece of my heart now, baby.
Have a!
Have another little piece of my heart now, baby.
You know you got it if it makes you feel good.

You're out in the street lookin' good,
And you know deep down in your heart that ain't right.
And oh, you never, never hear me when I cry at night.
Whoa-oh-oh.
I tell myself that I can't stand the pain,
But when you hold me in your arms I say it again.

Refrain

Point of Know Return

Words and Music by Steve Walsh, Phil Ehart and Robert Steinhardt

recorded by Kansas

I heard the men saying something.
The captains tell
They pay you well.
And they say they need sailing men
To show the way
And leave today.
Was it you that said,
"How long? How long?"

They say the sea turns so dark that
You know it's time
You see the sign.
They say the point demons guard
Is an ocean grave
For all the brave.
Was it you that said,
"How long? How long?"

"How long to the point of know return?"

Your father, he said he needs you.
Your mother, she said she loves you.
Your brothers, they echo the words
"How far to the point of know return,
To the point of know return?
Well, how long?
How long?"

Today I found a message floating
In the sea
From you to me.
You wrote that when you could see it,
You cried with fear
The point was near.
Was it you that said,
"How long? How long?"

"How long to the point of know return,
    know return?
How long?"

The Pusher

Words and Music by Hoyt Axton

recorded by Steppenwolf

You know, I've smoked a lot of grass,
Oh, Lord, I've popped a lot of pills.
But I never touched nothin'
That my spirit could kill.
You know, I've seen a lot of people walkin' 'round
With tombstones in their eyes.
But the pusher don't care,
Oh, if you live or if you die.

Refrain:
God damn the pusher.
God damn, hey, hey, I say, the pusher.
I say, God damn, God damn the pusher man.

You know the dealer, the dealer is a man
With the love grass in his hand.
Oh, but the pusher is a monster.
Good God, he's not a nat'ral man.
The dealer for a nickel,
Lord, he'll sell you lots of sweet dreams.
Ah, but the pusher'll ruin your body.
Lord, he'll leave your, he'll leave your mind to scream.

Refrain

Well, now if I were the president of this land,
You know I'd declare total war on the pusher man.
I'd cut him if he stands, and I'd shoot him if he'd run.
Then I'd kill him with my Bible and my razor and my gun.

Refrain

Question

Words and Music by Justin Hayward

recorded by The Moody Blues

Why do we never get an answer
When we're knocking at the door
With a thousand million questions
About hate and death and war?

'Cause when we stop and look around us
There is nothing that we need
In a world of persecution
That is burning in it's greed.

Why do we never get an answer
When we're knocking at the door?
Because the truth is hard to swallow,
That's what the war of love is for!

It's not the way that you say it
When you do those things to me.
It's more the way that you mean it
When you tell me what will be.

And when you stop, think about it.
You won't believe it's true.
That all the love you've been giving
Has all been meant for you.

I'm looking for someone to change my life.
I'm looking for a miracle in my life.
And if you could see what it's done to me,
To lose the love I knew
Could safely lead me through.

Between the silence of the mountains
And the crashing of the sea
There lies a land I once lived in
And she's waiting there for me.

But in the gray of the morning
My mind becomes confused
Between the dead and the sleeping
And the road that I must choose.

I'm looking for someone to change my life.
I'm looking for a miracle in my life.
And if you could see what it's done to me,
To lose the love I knew
Could safely lead me to
The land that I once knew,
To learn as we grow old
The secrets of your soul.

It's not the way that you say it
When you do those things to me.
It's more the way you really mean it
When you tell me what will be.

Why do we never get an answer
When we're knocking at the door
With a thousand million questions
About hate and death and war?

Why do we never get an answer
When we're knocking at the door?

Radar Love

Words and Music by George Kooymans and Barry Hay

recorded by Golden Earring

I've been drivin' all night. My hand's wet on
   the wheel.
There's a voice in my head that drives
   my heel.
It's my baby callin', said, "I need you here."
And it's half past four and I'm shiftin' gear.

When she is lonely and the longing gets too
   much,
She sends a cable coming in from above.
Don't need to phone at all.
We've got a thing that's called radar love.
We've got a wave in the air, radar love.

The radio was playin' some forgotten song.
Brenda Lee is comin' on strong.
The road has got me hypnotized,
And I'll be spitting into a new sunrise.

When I get lonely and I'm sure I've had
   enough,
She sends a comfort coming in from above.
We don't need no letter at all.
We've got a thing that's called radar love.
We've got an eye in the sky, radar love.

No more speed, I'm almost there.
I gotta keep cool now, gotta take care.
Last car to pass, here I go.
And the line of cars drove down real slow.

The radio played that forgotten song.
Brenda Lee is comin' on strong.
And the newsman sang his same song,
One more radar lover is gone.

When I get lonely and I'm sure I've had
   enough,
She sends a comfort coming in from above.
Don't need no letter at all.
We've got a thing that's called radar love.
We've got an eye in the sky.
We've got a thing that's called radar love.
We've got a thing that's called radar love.

Ramblin' Man

Words and Music by Dickey Betts

recorded by The Allman Brothers Band

Refrain:
Lord, I was born a ramblin' man,
Try'n' to make a livin' and doin' the best I can.
And when it's time for leavin', I hope you'll understand
That I was born a ramblin' man.

Well, my father was a gambler down in Georgia,
And he wound up on the wrong end of a gun.
And I was born in the back seat of a Greyhound bus
Rollin' down Highway 41.

Refrain

I'm on my way to New Orleans this mornin',
Leavin' out of Nashville, Tennessee.
They're always havin' a good time down on the bayou, Lord,
Them delta women think the world of me.

Refrain

Lord, I was born a ramblin' man.

Rebel, Rebel

Words and Music by David Bowie

recorded by David Bowie

Got your mother in a whirl,
She's not sure if you're a boy or a girl.
Hey, babe, your hair's alright.
Hey, babe, let's go out tonight.
You like me and I like it all,
We like dancing and we look divine.
You love bands when they play it hard,
You want more and you want it fast.
Put you down and say I'm wrong,
You tacky thing, and put them on.

Refrain:
Rebel, rebel, you've torn your dress.
Rebel, rebel, your face is a mess.
Rebel, rebel, how could they know,
Hot tramp, I love you so.
Don't you?

Got your mother in a whirl,
'Cause she's not sure if you're a boy or a girl.
Hey, babe, your hair's alright.
Hey, babe, let's stay out tonight.
You like me and I like it all,
We like dancing and we look divine.
You love bands when they play it hard,
You want more and you want it fast.
Put you down and say I'm wrong,
You tacky thing, and put them on.

Refrain Twice

You've torn your dress, your face is a mess.
You can't get enough, but enough ain't
    the test.
Transmission and a live wire,
You got your cue lines and a handful
    of ludes.
You wanna danger when they count out
    the pews.
But you love your dress, you're a juvenile
    success,
Because your face is a mess.
So how could they know,
I said, how could they know?
But you wanna know.

Refugee

Words and Music by Tom Petty and Mike Campbell

recorded by Tom Petty and The Heartbreakers

We got somethin', we both know it,
We don't talk too much about it.
Ain't no real big secret, all the same,
Somehow, we get around it.
Listen, it don't really matter to me, baby.
You believe what you want to believe.
You see, you don't have to live like a refugee.

Somewhere, somehow, somebody
Must have kicked you around some.
Tell me why you want to lay there,
Revel in your abandon.
Honey, it don't make no diff'rence to me, baby.
Ev'rybody's had to fight to be free.
You see, you don't have to live like a refugee.
No, baby, you don't have to live like a refugee.

Baby, we ain't the first.
I'm sure a lot of other lovers been burned.
Right now this seems real to you,
But it's one of those things you gotta feel to be true.

Somewhere, somehow, somebody
Must have kicked you around some.
Who knows? Maybe you were kidnapped, tied up,
Taken away, and held for ransom.
Honey, it don't really matter to me, baby.
Ev'rybody's had to fight to be free.
You see, you don't have to live like a refugee.
No, baby, you don't have to live like a refugee.
Baby, you don't have to live like a refugee.

Revolution

Words and Music by John Lennon and Paul McCartney

recorded by The Beatles

You say you want a revolution
Well, you know
We all want to change the world
You tell me that it's evolution
Well, you know
We all want to change the world
But when you talk about destruction
Don't you know that you can count me out
Don't you know it's going to be alright
Alright, alright

You say you want a real solution
Well, you know
We'd all love to see the plan
You ask me for a contribution
Well, you know
We're doing what we can
But if you want money for people with minds that hate
All I can tell you is brother you have to wait
Don't you know it's going to be alright
Alright, alright

You say you'll change the Constitution
Well, you know
We all want to change your head
You tell me it's the institution
Well, you know
You better free your mind instead
But if you carrying pictures of Chairman Mao
You ain't going to make it with me anyhow
Don't you know it's going to be alright
Alright, alright
Alright, alright…

Rhiannon

Words and Music by Stevie Nicks

recorded by Fleetwood Mac

Rhiannon rings like a bell through the night,
And wouldn't you love to love her?
Takes to the sky like a bird in flight
And who will be her lover?

Refrain:
All your life you've never seen a woman
Taken by the wind.
Would you stay if she promised you heaven?
Will you ever win?
Will you ever win?

She is like a cat in the dark,
And then she is the darkness.
She rules her life like a fine skylark,
And when the sky is starless.

Refrain

Rhiannon.
Rhiannon.

Repeat and Fade:
Dreams unwind; love's a state of mind.

Ridin' the Storm Out

Words and Music by Gary Richrath

recorded by REO Speedwagon

Ridin' the storm out,
Waitin' for the thaw out
On a full moon night in the Rocky Mountain winter.
Wine bottle's low
Watching for the snow
And thinkin' about what I've been missin' in the city.

Refrain:
And I'm not missin' a thing,
Watching the full moon crossin' the range.
Ridin' the storm out. Ridin' the storm out.
Ridin' the storm out. Ridin' the storm out.

Lady beside me,
Well, she's there to guide me.
She says that alone we've finally found our home.
Well, the wind outside is frightenin',
But it's kinder than lightnin' life in the city.
A hard life to live, but it gives back what you give.

Refrain

Whoa, yes, I am.

Repeat Verse 1

Refrain

Oh no. Oh no. Oh, oh, oh, oh.

Rock and Roll Hoochie Koo

Words and Music by Rick Derringer

recorded by Rick Derringer

I couldn't stop moving when it first
   took hold.
It was a warm spring night at the old
   town hall.
There was a band called the Jokers,
   they were laying it down.
But you know I'm never gonna lose
   that funky sound.

Rock and roll hoochie koo.
(Rock and roll hoochie koo.)
Truck on out and spread the news,

Mosquitos started buzzin' 'bout this time
   of year.
I'm going out back, said she'll meet
   me there.
We were rollin' in the grass that
   grows behind the barn
When my ears started ringing like a
   fire alarm.

Refrain:
Rock and roll hoochie koo.
(Rock and roll hoochie koo.)
Lordy, mama, light my fuse.
Rock and roll hoochie koo.
(Rock and roll hoochie koo.)
Truck on out and spread the news.

I hope you all know what I'm talkin' about.
The way they wiggle that thing really
   knocks me out.
Gettin' high all the time, hope you
   all are too.
Come on a little closer, gonna do it to you.

Refrain

(Rock and roll hoochie koo.)
That I'm tired of payin' dues.
(Rock and roll hoochie koo.)
Done said good-bye to all my blues.
(Rock and roll hoochie koo.)
Lordy, mama, light my fuse.

Rockin' into the Night

Words and Music by Frank Sullivan, Jim Peterik and Robert Gary Smith

recorded by .38 Special

Cruisin' down the motorway, got my girl by
  my side.
We're both a little anxious, oo, we got love
  on our mind.

Waiting, anticipating, for the fireworks in
  the night.
Well, I swear we were doin' eighty
When we saw those motel lights.
And we were rockin' into the night,
Rockin' into the night, yeah...
Out on the back street, taking love where I
  can,
I found a sweet Madonna, oo, with a Bible
  in her hand.
She's waiting, anticipating,
Well, for someone to save her soul.
Well, I ain't no new messiah,
But I'm close enough for rock and roll.

And we were rockin' into the night,
Rockin' into the night.
Rockin' into the night.

And she's pullin' in yes, she's pullin' in.

Waiting, anticipating for the fireworks in the
  night.
Well, I swear we were doin' eighty
When we saw those motel lights.
We were rockin', rockin' into the night,
Ooo, Yeah...
We were rockin', rockin' into the night,
Ooo, Yeah...
Rockin' into the night, rockin' into the night,
Hoo, rockin'!

Roxanne

Written and Composed by Sting

recorded by The Police

Roxanne, you don't have to put on the red light.
Those days are over;
You don't have to sell your body to the night.
Roxanne, you don't have to wear that dress tonight,
Walk the streets for money;
You don't care if it's wrong or if it's right.

Refrain:
Roxanne, you don't have to put on the red light.
Roxanne, you don't have to put on the red light.
Roxanne, (Put on the red light.)

I loved you since I knew ya.
I wouldn't talk down to ya.
I have to tell you just how I feel:
I won't share you with another boy.
I know my mind is made up,
So, put away your makeup.
Told you once I won't tell you again,
It's a crime by the way…

Refrain

Run to You

Words and Music by Bryan Adams and Jim Vallance

recorded by Bryan Adams

She says her love for me could never die.
But that'd change if she ever found out
    about you and I.
Oh, but her love is cold.
Wouldn't hurt her if she didn't know,
'Cause when it gets too much,
I need to feel your touch.

Refrain:
I'm gonna run to you.
I'm gonna run to you.
'Cause when the feeling's right,
I'm gonna run all night,
I'm gonna run to you.

She's got a heart of gold, she'd never let
    me down.
But you're the one that always turns me on,
You keep me comin' 'round.
I know her love is true, but it's so damn
    easy makin' love to you.
I got my mind made up,
I need to feel your touch.

Refrain

Yeah, I'm gonna run to you.
Oh, when the feeling's right,
I'm gonna run all night,
I'm gonna run to you.
When the feeling's right, now.

Refrain

Oh, I'm gonna run to you.
Yeah, and when the feeling's right,
I'm gonna stay all night,
I'm gonna run to you.
Oh, when the feeling's right, now.

Runnin' Down a Dream

Words and Music by Jeff Lynne, Tom Petty and Mike Campbell

recorded by Tom Petty

It was a beautiful day, the sun beat down.
I had the radio on; I was drivin'.
The trees flew by. Me and Del were singin'
Little "Runaway." I was flyin'.

Refrain:
Yeah, runnin' down a dream
That never would come to me.
Workin' on a mystery;
Goin' wherever it leads.
Runnin' down a dream.

I felt so good, like anything is possible,
Hit cruise control and rubbed my eyes.
The last three days the rain was unstoppable.
It was always cold, no sunshine.

Refrain

I rolled on, the sky grew dark.
I put the pedal down to make some time.
There's something good waitin' down this road.
I'm pickin' up whatever's mine.

Refrain

Running on Faith

Words and Music by Jerry Williams

recorded by Eric Clapton

Lately I've been running on faith,
What else can a poor boy do?
But my world would be right
When love comes over you.

Lately I've been talking in my sleep,
Can't imagine what I'd have to say,
Except my world will be right
When love comes back your way.

Refrain:
I've always been
One to take each and ev'ry day.
Seems like by now,
I've found a love who cares just for me.

Then we'd go running on faith,
All of our dreams will come true.
And our world will be right
When love comes over me and you.

Refrain

Then we'd go running on faith,
All of our dreams will come true.
And the world will be right
When love comes over you.
When love comes over you.

School's Out

Words and Music by Alice Cooper, Neal Smith, Michael Bruce, Glen Buxton and Dennis Dunaway

recorded by Alice Cooper

Well, we got no choice,
All the girls and boys
Makin' all their noise
'Cause they found new toys.
Well, we can't salute ya,
Can't find a flag.
If that don't suit ya,
That's a drag.

School's out for summer!
School's out forever!
School's been blown to pieces!

No more pencils, no more books,
No more teacher's dirty looks.

Well, we got no class,
And we got no principles,
And we got no innocence.
We can't even think of a word that rhymes!

School's out for summer!
School's out forever!
My school's been blown to pieces!

No more pencils, no more books,
No more teacher's dirty looks.
Out for summer, out till fall.
We might not go back at all!

School's out forever!
School's out for summer!
School's out with fever!
School's out completely!

Shakedown

Words and Music by Keith Forsey, Harold Faltermeyer and Bob Seger

recorded by Bob Seger
from the Paramount Motion Picture *Beverly Hills Cop II*

No matter what you think you've pulled,
You'll find it's not enough.
No matter who you think you know,
You won't get through.
It's a given L.A. law;
Someone's faster on the draw.
No matter where you hide,
I'm comin' after you.

No matter how the race is run,
It always ends the same.
Another room without a view
Awaits downtown.
You can shake me for a while;
Live it up in style.
No matter what you do,
I'm going to take you down.

Refrain:
Shakedown, breakdown, takedown;
Everybody wants into the crowded light.
Breakdown, takedown; you're busted.
Let down your guard, honey,
Just about the time you think that it's alright.
Breakdown, takedown; you're busted.

This is the town where ev'ryone
Is reachin' for the top.
This is a place where second best
Will never do.
It's OK to want to shine,
But once you step across that line,
No matter where you hide,
I'm comin' after you.

Shakedown, breakdown, takedown;
Everybody wants into the crowded light.
Breakdown, takedown; you're busted.
Shakedown, breakdown; honey,
Just about the time you think that it's alright.
Breakdown, takedown; you're busted.

Shattered

Words and Music by Mick Jagger and Keith Richards

recorded by The Rolling Stones

Uh huh. Shattered. Uh huh. Shattered.

Spoken:
Love and hope and sex and dreams
Are still survivin' on the streets.
Look at me!
I'm in tatters.
I been shattered.

Sung:
Shattered.

Spoken:
Friends are so alarming and my lover's
　　never charming.
Life's just a cocktail party on the street.
Big Apple people dressed in plastic bags
　　directing traffic.
Some kind-a fashion.

Sung:
Shattered.

Spoken:
Laughter, joy and loneliness
And sex, and sex, and sex, and sex and
Look at me!
I'm in tatters.
I'm a-shattered.

Sung:
Shattered.

Spoken:
All this chitter chatter, chitter chatter,
Chitter chatter, 'bout shmatter,
　　shmatter, shmatter.
I can't give it away on Seventh Avenue.
This town's been wearin' tatters. Uh huh.

Sung:
Sah-doo-bee. Shattered.

Spoken:
Work and work for love and sex.
Ain't you hungry for success?
Success, success, success!
Does it matter? I'm shattered.
Does it matter?
Pride and joy and greed and sex,
That's what makes our town the best.
Pride and joy and dirty dreams
Are still survivin' on the streets and
　　look at me!
I'm in tatters. Yeah! I been battered.
What does it matter? What does it matter?
Uh huh, does it matter?

Uh huh, I'm a-shattered.
Mm. I'm shattered.

Sung:
Sha-doo-bee.

Spoken:
Shattered.
Don't you know the crime rate's goin'
Up, up, up, up, up?
To live in this town you must be
Tough, tough, tough, tough, tough, tough, tough.
My brain's been battered,
Splattered all over Manhattan.
Uh huh. What say?

Sung:
Sha-doo-bee. Shattered. Sha-doo-bee.
Shattered Sha-doo-bee.
Uh huh. This town's full of money grabbers.
Go ahead! Bite the Big Apple.
Don't mind the maggots!

Uh huh. Shattered. Sah-doo-bee.
My brain's been battered!
My family came around 'n' flatter, flatter,
Flatter, flatter, flatter, flatter, flatter.
Pile it up! Pile it up!
Pile it high on the platter.

She's So Cold

Words and Music by Mick Jagger and Keith Richards

recorded by The Rolling Stones

I'm so hot for her, I'm so hot for her,
I'm so hot for her and she's so cold.
I'm so hot for her, I'm so hot for her,
I'm so hot for her and she's so cold.
I'm a burning bush, I'm the burning fire,
I'm the bleeding volcano.
I'm so hot for her, I'm so hot for her,
I'm so hot for her and she's so cold.

Yes, I've tried rewiring her, tried
    refiring her,
I think her engine is permanently stalled.
She's so cold, she's so cold,
She's so cold, cold, cold,
Like a tomb of stone.
She's so cold, she's so cold,
She's so cold, cold, cold,
Like an ice cream cone.
She's so cold, she's so cold,
When I touched her my hand just froze.

I'm so hot for her, I'm so hot for her,
I'm so hot for her, she's so cold.
Put your hand on the heat, put your hand
    on the heat,
I'm coming on baby let's go, go.
She's so cold, she's so cold, cold, she's so
    c,c,c,c,cold,
But she's beautiful.

She's so cold.
She's so cold, she's so cold,
I think she was born in an arctic zone.
She's so cold, she's so cold, cold, cold.
When I touched her, my hand just froze.
She's so cold, she's so god-damn cold,
She's so cold, cold, cold,
She's so cold.

Who will believe you were a beauty indeed,
When the days get shorter and the
    nights get long?
Light fades and the rain comes;
Nobody will know
When you're old, when your old,
Nobody will know that you was a beauty,
A sweet, sweet, beauty, a sweet, sweet beauty,
But stone, stone cold.
You're so cold, You're so cold, cold, cold.
You're so cold, you're so cold.
I'm so hot for you, I'm so hot for you,
I'm so hot for you and you're so cold.

Repeat and Fade:
I'm a burning bush, I'm the burning fire,
I'm the bleeding volcano.

Show Me the Way

Words and Music by Peter Frampton

recorded by Peter Frampton

I wonder how you're feeling,
There's ringing in my ears.
And no one to relate to 'cept the sea.
Who can I believe in?
I'm kneeling on the floor.
There has to be a force, who do I phone?
The stars are out and shining,
But all I really wanna know,

Oh, won't you show me the way, ev'ry day.
I want you to show me the way, yeah.

Well, I can see no reason,
You living on your nerves,
When someone drops a cup and I
   submerge.
I'm swimming in a circle,
I feel I'm going down.
There has to be a fool to play my part.
Someone thought of healing,
But all I really wanna know,

Oh, won't you show me the way, ev'ry day.
I want you to show me the way.
Oh, I want you day after day, hey.

And I wonder if I'm dreaming,
I feel so unashamed.
I can't believe this is happening to me.
I watch you when you're sleeping,
Oh, then I wanna take your love.

Oh, won't you show me the way, ev'ry day.
I want you to show me the way,
   one more time.
I want you day after day, hey.
I want you day after day, hey.

I want you to show me the way, ev'ry day.
I want you to show me the way,
   night and day.
I want you day after day, hey, hey, oh.

Sign of the Gypsy Queen

Words and Music by Lorence Hud

recorded by April Wine

Lightning smokes on the hill rise
Brought the man with the warnin' light,
Shoutin' loud, "You had better fly
While the darkness can help you hide."
Troubles comin' without control;
No one's stayin' who's got a hope.
Hurricane at the very least,
In the words of the gypsy queen.

Refrain:
Sign of the gypsy queen;
Pack your things and leave.
Word of a woman who knows:
"Take all your gold, and you go."

Get my saddle and tie it on
Western Wind, who is fast and strong.
Jump on back, he is good and long;
We'll resist till he reach the dawn.
Runnin' seems like the best defense;
Staying just don't make any sense.
No one could ever stop it now;
Show the cards of the gypsy town.

Refrain

Shadows movin' without a sound
From the hold of his sleepless town.
Evil seems to be ev'rywhere;
Heed the spirit that brought despair.
Troubles comin' without control;
No one's stayin' that's got a hope.
Hurricane at the very least,
In the words of the gypsy queen.

Refrain

Smoke on the Water

Words and Music by Ritchie Blackmore, Ian Gillan, Roger Glover, Jon Lord and Ian Paice

recorded by Deep Purple

We all came to Montreux
On the Lake Geneva shoreline
To make records with the mobile,
We didn't have much time.
But Frank Zappa and the Mothers
Were at the best place around.
But some stupid with a flare gun
Burned the place to the ground.

Refrain:
Smoke on the water, a fire in the sky.
Smoke on the water.

They burned down the gambling house,
It died with an awful sound.
A funky Claude was running in and out,
Pulling kids on the ground.
When it all was over,
We had to find another place.
But Swiss time was running out,
It seemed that we would lose the race.

Refrain

We ended up at the Grand Hotel,
It was empty, cold and bare.
But with the Rollin Truck Stones thing just outside,
Making our music there.
With a few red lights, a few old beds,
We made a place to sweat.
No matter what we got out of this,
I know we'll never forget.

Refrain

So into You

Words and Music by Buddy Buie, Dean Daughtry and Robert Nix

recorded by Atlanta Rhythm Section

When you walked into the room
There was voodoo in the vibes.
I was captured by your style,
But I could not catch your eyes.
Now I stand here helplessly,
Hoping you'll be into me.

I am so into you.
I can't think of nothing else.
I am so into you.
I can't think of nothing else.

Thinking how it's going to be
Whenever I get you next to me.
It's gonna be good.
Don't you know, from your head to your toe,
Gonna love you all over, over and over.
Me into you, you into me, me into you.

Repeat Verse 1

I am so into you.
I can't get to nothing else.
I am so into you.
I can't get to nothing else.

Come on, baby.
I'm so into you.
Love the things you do.
Listen, baby.
Driving me crazy.
I'm so into you.
Love the things you do.

(She's) Some Kind of Wonderful

Words and Music by John Ellison

recorded by Grand Funk Railroad

I don't need a whole lot's of money.
I don't need a big fine car.
I got everything that a man could want.
I got more then I could ask for.
I, I don't have to run around.
I don't have to stay out all night.
'Cause I got me a sweet, sweet lovin' woman
And she knows just how to treat me right.

Refrain:
Well, my baby, she's alright.
She's clean out of sight.
Don't you know that she's,
She's some kind of wonderful.
She's some kind of wonderful.
Yeah, she is, she's some kind of wonderful.
Yeah, yeah, yeah, yeah.

When I hold her in my arms,
You know she sets my soul on fire.
Ooh, when my baby kisses me
My heart becomes filled with desire.
When she wraps her lovin' arms around me
It about drives me out of my mind.
Yeah, when my baby kisses me
Chills run up and down my spine.

Refrain

Now is there anybody
Got a sweet little woman like mine?
There's got to be somebody
Got a sweet little woman like mine.
Yeah. Now can I witness?
Can I get a witness?
Well, can I get a witness?
Can I get a witness?
Can I get a witness?
Can I get a witness?
I'm talkin', talkin' 'bout my baby.

Repeat and Fade:
She's some kind of wonderful.
Talkin' 'bout my baby.
She's some kind of wonderful.

Something to Talk About
(Let's Give Them Something to Talk About)

Words and Music by Shirley Eikhard

recorded by Bonnie Raitt
featured in the film *Something to Talk About*

People are talking,
Talking about people.
I hear them whisper,
"You won't believe it."
They think we're lovers
Kept undercover.
I just ignore it.
They keep saying we
Laugh just a little too loud,
Stand just a little too close,
We stare just a little too long.
Maybe they're seeing something we don't,
    darling.

Let's give them something to talk about.
Let's give them something to talk about.
I wanna give them something to talk about.
I want your love.

I feel so foolish.
I never noticed that,
Baby, you're acting so nervous
Like you're falling.
It took a rumor
To make me wonder.
Now I'm convinced that
You're going under, now.
Thinking about you every day,
Dreaming about you every night,
Hoping that you feel the same way.
Now that we know it, let's really show it,
    baby.

Come on, give them something to talk about.
A little mystery to figure out.
I wanna give them something to talk about,
Talk about love.

Give a little something to talk about
I got some mystery, why don't you just
    figure out.
Give them something to talk about.
How about love?
Listen up, baby.
A little mystery won't hurt.
Give them something to talk about.
How about love?

Space Oddity

Words and Music by David Bowie

recorded by David Bowie

Ground Control to Major Tom.
Ground Control to Major Tom.
Take your protein pills and put your
  helmet on.
Ground Control to Major Tom.
(*Spoken:* Ten, nine, eight, seven, six,)
commencing countdown, engines on.
(five, four, three, two, one, liftoff.)
Checking ignition and may God's love
  be with you.

This is Ground Control to Major Tom,
You've really made the grade.
And the papers want to know whose
  shirts you wear.
Now it's time to leave the capsule
  if you dare.

This is Major Tom to Ground Control,
I'm stepping through the door.
And I'm floating in a most peculiar way.
And the stars look very different today.

For here am I sitting in a tin can,
Far above the world.
Planet Earth is blue, and there's nothing
  I can do.

Though I'm past one hundred thousand
  miles,
I'm feeling very still.
And I think my spaceship knows which
  way to go.
Tell my wife I love her very much.
  She knows.

Ground Control to Major Tom,
Your circuit's dead, there's something wrong.
Can you hear me Major Tom?
Can you hear me Major Tom?
Can you hear me Major Tom?
Can you...

Here am I floating 'round my tin can,
Far above the world.
Planet Earth is blue, and there's nothing
  I can do.

Start Me Up

Words and Music by Mick Jagger and Keith Richards

recorded by The Rolling Stones

If you start me up, if you start me up,
I'll never stop.
You can start me up, you can start me up,
I'll never stop.
I've been running hot;
You got me just about to blow my top.

You can start me up. you can start me up,
I never stop, never stop, never stop,
    never stop.
You make a grown man cry.
You make a grown man cry.
You make a grown man cry.
Spread out the oil, the gasoline.
I walk smooth, ride in a mean, mean
    machine.
Start it up.

You can start me up, kick on the starter,
Give it all you've got.
I can't compete with riders in the
    other heats.
You can rough it up, if you like it
You can slide it up, slide it up, slide it up,
    slide it up.
Don't make a grown man cry.
My eyes dilate, my lips go green,
My hands are greasy, she's a mean, mean
    machine.
Start it up.

Start me up,
Ah, you've got to, you've got to,
Never, never, never stop.
You make a grown man cry.
You make a grown man cry.
You make a grown man cry.
Ride like the wind, at double speed.
I'll take you places that you've never,
    never seen.
If you start it up,
Love the day when we will never stop,
Never stop, never, never, never stop.

The Story in Your Eyes

Words and Music by Justin Hayward

recorded by The Moody Blues

I've been thinking 'bout our fortune,
And I've decided that we're really not to blame,
For the love that's deep inside us now is still the same.

And the sound we make together
Is the music to the story in your eyes.
It's been shining down upon you now, I realize.

Refrain:
Listen to the tide slowly turning.
Wash all our heartaches away.
We're part of a fire that is burning,
And from the ashes we can build another day.

But I'm frightened for your children,
That the life that we are living is in vain,
And the sunshine we've been waiting for will turn to rain.

Refrain

But I'm frightened for your children,
That the life that we are living is in vain,
And the sunshine we've been waiting for will turn to rain.

When the final line is over,
And it's certain that the curtain's gonna fall,
I can hide inside your sweet, sweet love forevermore.

Strange Brew

Words and Music by Eric Clapton, Felix Pappalardi and Gail Collins

recorded by Cream

Strange brew, killing what's inside of you.

She's a witch of trouble in electric blue.
, In her own mad mind she's in love with you, with you.
Now what you gonna do?
Strange brew, killing what's inside of you.

She's some kind of demon dusting in the flue,
If you don't watch out, it'll stick to you, to you.
What kind of fool are you?
Strange brew, killing what's inside of you.
On a boat in the middle of a raging sea,
She would make a scene for it all to be ignored.
And wouldn't you be bored?
Strange brew, killing what's inside of you.

Suffragette City

Words and Music by David Bowie

recorded by David Bowie

(Hey, man) Oh, leave me alone, you know.
(Hey, man) Oh, Henry, get off the phone,
   I gotta
(Hey, man) I gotta straighten my face,
This mellow-thighed chick just put my
   spine out of place.

(Hey, man) My school day's insane.
(Hey, man) My work's down the drain.
(Hey, man) Well, she's a total blam-blam.
She said she had to squeeze it but she—
   and then she—

Refrain:
Oh, don't lean on me, man,
'Cause you can't afford the ticket.
I'm back on Suffragette City.
No, don't lean on me, man,
'Cause you ain't got time to check it.
You know my Suffragette City
Is outta sight. She's alright.

(Hey, man) Ah Henry, don't be unkind,
   go away.
(Hey, man) I can't take you this time,
   no way.
(Hey, man) Droogie don't crash here.
There's only room for one and here she
   comes, here she comes.

Refrain

Repeat Ad Lib:
A Suffragette City, a Suffragette City.

Suffragette.

Suite: Judy Blue Eyes

Words and Music by Stephen Stills

recorded by Crosby, Stills & Nash

It's getting to the point
Where I'm no fun anymore.
I am sorry.
Sometimes it hurts
So badly I must cry out loud.
I am lonely.

Refrain:
I am yours, you are mine,
You are what you are.
You make it hard.

Remember what we've said
And done and felt about each other.
Oh, babe, have mercy.
Don't let the past
Remind us of what we are not now.
I am not dreaming.

Refrain

Tearing yourself away from me now,
You are free, and I am crying.
This does not mean I don't love you,
I do, that's forever, yes, and for always.

Refrain

Something inside
Is telling me that I've got your secret.
Are you still list'ning?
Fear is the lock
And laughter the key to your heart,
And I love you.

Refrain

And you make it hard,
And you make it hard,
And you make it hard.

Friday evening, Sunday in the afternoon.
What have you got to lose?
Tuesday morning, please be gone,
   I'm tired of you.
What have you got to lose?
Can I tell it like it is?
But listen to me, baby.
It's my heart that's a-suff'rin'. It's a-dyin'.
And that's what I have to lose.

I've got an answer. I'm going to fly away.
What have I got to lose?
Will you come see me Thursdays
   and Saturdays?
What have you got to lose?

Chestnut-brown canary, ruby-throated sparrow.
Sing a song, don't be long,
Thrill me to the marrow.

Voices of the angels, ring around the moonlight.
Asking me, said, "She so free,
How can you catch the sparrow?"

Lacy, lilting lyric, losing love, lamenting,
Change my life, make it right.
Be my lady.

Twice:
Do do do do do,
Do do do do do do.
Do do do do do,
Do do do do.

Que linda me la traiga Cuba,
La reina de la Mar Caribe.
Cielo sol no tiene sangre ahí,
Y que triste que no puedo vaya.
Oh va! Oh va!

Twice:
Do do do do do,
Do do do do do do.
Do do do do do,
Do do do do.

Sultans of Swing

Words and Music by Mark Knopfler

recorded by Dire Straits

You get a shiver in the dark, it's raining in
the park, but meantime,
South of the river you stop and you hold
ev'rything.
A band is blowin' Dixie double four time.
You feel all right when you hear the music
ring.

Well, now, you step inside but you don't see
too many faces
Comin' in out of the rain, they hear the jazz
go down.
Competition in other places,
But the horns, they blowin' that sound.
Way on down south, way on down south
London town.

You check out Guitar George, he knows all
the chords.
Mind, he's strictly rhythm, he doesn't want
to make it cry or sing.
Yes, and an old guitar is just all he can
afford,
When he gets up under the lights to play his
thing.

And Harry doesn't mind if he doesn't make
the scene.
He's got a daytime job, he's doing alright.
He can play the honky-tonk like anything,
Savin' it up, Friday night
With the Sultans, with the Sultans of Swing.

And a crowd of young boys, they're foolin'
around in the corner,
Drunk and dressed in their best brown
baggies, and their platform soles.
They don't give a damn about any trumpet-
playin' band;
It ain't what they call rock and roll.
And the Sultans, yeah, the Sultans are playing
Creole.

And then the man, he steps right up to the
microphone
And says at last, just as the time-bell rings:
"Good night, now it's time to go home."
Then he makes it fast with one more thing:
"We are the Sultans, we are the Sultans of
Swing."

THE LYRIC LIBRARY

Sunshine of Your Love

Words and Music by Jack Bruce, Pete Brown and Eric Clapton

recorded by Cream

It's getting near dawn when lights close their tired eyes.
I'll soon be with you, my love,
To give you my dawn surprise,
I'll be with you darling, soon.
I'll be with you when the stars start falling.

I've been waiting so long to be where I'm going
In the sunshine of your love.

I'm with you my love; the light shining through on you.
Yes, I'm with you, my love.
It's the morning and just we two.
I'll stay with you darling, now,
I'll stay with you till my seeds are dried up.

I've been waiting so long,
I've been waiting so long,
I've been waiting so long to be where I'm going
In the sunshine of your love.

Surrender

Words and Music by Rick Nielsen

recorded by Cheap Trick

Mother told me, yes, she told me, I'd meet girls like you.
She also told me, "Stay away, you'll never know what you'll catch.
Just the other day I heard of a soldier's falling off
Some Indonesian junk that's going 'round."

Refrain:
Mommy's all right, Daddy's all right,
They just seem a little weird.
Surrender, surrender,
But don't give yourself away, way, way.

Father says, "Your mother's right, she's really up on things.
Before we married, Mommy served in the WACs in the Philippines."
Now I had heard the WACs recruited old maids for the war.
But Mommy isn't one of those, I've known her all these years.

Refrain

Whatever happened to all this season's losers of the year?
Ev'ry time I got to thinking, where'd they disappear.
When I woke up, Mom and Dad are rolling on the couch.
Rolling numbers, rock and rolling, got my Kiss records out.

Refrain

Away.
Away.
Surrender, surrender,
But don't give yourself away.

Sussudio

Words and Music by Phil Collins

recorded by Phil Collins

There's a girl that's been on my mind
All the time,
Su Sussudio, oh, oh.
Now she don't even know my name,
But I think she likes me just the same,
Su Sussudio, oh, oh.
Ah, if she called me I'd be there.
I'd come running anywhere.

Refrain:
She's all I need, all my life.
I feel so good
If I just say the word,
Su Sussudio.
Just say the word, oh, Sussudio.

Now I know that I'm too young,
My life has just begun,
Su Sussudio, oh, oh.
Ooh, give me a chance,
Give me a sign,
I'll show her anytime,
Su Sussudio, oh, oh.
Ah, I've got to have her,
Have her now.
I've got to get closer but I don't know how.
She makes me nervous and makes me
    scared,
But I'll feel so good…

Refrain

I'll just say the word,
Su Sussudio.
Just say the word, oh, Sussudio.

Just say the word.
Ooh, just, just, just say the word.
Just say the word.
Su Su Sussudio.
Su Sussudio.
Su Sussudio.
Su Sussudio, sudio, Su Sussudio
Just say the word.
Su Sussudio.
Say the word…

Sweet Emotion

Words and Music by Steven Tyler and Tom Hamilton

recorded by Aerosmith

Sweet emotion. Sweet emotion.
You talk about things and nobody cares.
You wearin' out things that nobody wears.
You're callin' my name but I gotta make clear,
I can't say, baby, where I'll be in a year.
Some sweet talkin' mama with a face like a gent
Said my get-up-and-go must have got up and went.
Well I got good news, she's a real good liar
'Cause my back stage boogie set yo' pants on fire.

Sweet emotion, sweet emotion.
I pulled into town in a police car;
Your daddy said I took you just a little too far.
You're tellin' her things but your girlfriend lied;
You can't catch me 'cause the rabbit done died.
Stand in front just a-shakin' your ass;
I'll take you backstage, you can drink from my glass.
I'm talking 'bout somethin' you can sure understand,
'Cause a month on the road
And I'll be eatin' from your hand.

Repeat and Fade:
Sweet emotion, Sweet emotion.

Sweet Talkin' Woman

Words and Music by Jeff Lynne

recorded by Electric Light Orchestra

I was searchin' on a one-way street.
I was hopin' for a chance to meet.
I was waitin' for the operator on the line.
(She's gone so long.)
What can I do?
(Where could she be?)
Don't know what I'm gonna do.
I gotta get back to you.

Refrain:
(You gotta) Slow down, sweet talkin' woman.
You got me runnin', you got me searchin'.
Hold on, sweet talkin' lover,
It's so sad if that's the way it's over.

I was walkin', many days go by.
I was thinkin' 'bout the lonely nights.
Communication break down all around.
(She's gone so long.)
What can I do?
(Where could she be?)
Don't know what I'm gonna do.
I gotta get back to you.

Refrain

I've been livin' on a dead-end street.
I've been askin' ev'rybody I meet.
Insufficient data coming through.
(She's gone so long.)
What can I do?
(Where could she be?)
Don't know what I'm gonna do.
I gotta get back to you.

Refrain

Take the Long Way Home

Words and Music by Rick Davies and Roger Hodgson

recorded by Supertramp

So you think you're a Romeo
Playing a part in a picture show.
Well, take the long way home,
Take the long way home.
'Cause you're the joke of the neighborhood.
Why should you care if you're feeling good?
Well, take the long way home,
Take the long way home.

But there are times that you feel
You're part of the scenery.
All the greenery is comin' down, boy.
And then your wife seems to think
You're part of the furniture.
,Oh, it's peculiar, she used to be so nice.

When lonely days turn to lonely nights,
You take a trip to the city lights
And take the long way home,
Take the long way home.
You never see what you want to see,
Forever playing to the gallery.
You take the long way home,
Take the long way home.

And when you're up on the stage,
It's so unbelievable,
Unforgettable, how they adore you.
But then your wife seems to think
You're losing your sanity.
Oh, it's calamity, oh, is there no way out?

Does it feel that your life's become a
   catastrophe?
Oh, it has to be for you to grow, boy.
When you look through the years
And see what you could have been,
Oh, what you might have been
If you'd had more time.

So, when the day comes to settle down,
Well, who's to blame if you're not around?

Four Times:
You took the long way home,
You took the long way home.

Long way home, long way home,
   long way home.
Long way home, long way home,
   long way home.

Takin' Care of Business

Words and Music by Randy Bachman

recorded by Bachman-Turner Overdrive

They get up every mornin'
From the 'larm clock's warnin',
Take the eight-fifteen into the city.
There's a whistle up above and
People pushin', people shovin'
And the girls who try to look pretty.
And if your train's on time,
You can get to work by nine,
And start your slavin' job to get your pay.
If you ever get annoyed,
Look at me, I'm self-employed,
I love to work at nothin' all day.

Refrain:
And I've been takin' care of business,
Every day.
Takin' care of business,
Every way.
I've been takin' care of business
It's all mine,
Takin' care of business and workin'
    over-time,
Work out.

There's work easy as fishin',
You could be a musician
If you can make sounds loud or mellow.
Get a second-hand guitar,
Chances are you'll go far
If you get in with the right bunch of fellows.
People see you havin' fun,
Just a lyin' in the sun,
Tell them that you like it this way.
It's the work that we avoid
And we're all self-employed,
We love to work at nothin' all day.

Refrain

These Eyes

Written by Burton Cummings and Randy Bachman

recorded by The Guess Who

These eyes cry ev'ry night for you.
These arms long to hold you again.
The hurting's on me,
But I will never be free.
You gave a promise to me
And you broke it, and you broke it.

These eyes watched you bring my world to an end.
This heart could not accept and pretend.
The hurting's on me,
But I will never be free.
You took the vow with me
When you spoke it, when you spoke it.

Repeat Three Times:
These eyes are cryin'.
These eyes have seen a lot of love,
But they're never gonna see
Another one like I had with you.

Repeat Verse 2

Time

Words and Music by Roger Waters, Nicholas Mason, David Gilmour and Rick Wright

recorded by Pink Floyd

Ticking away the moments that make up a dull day.
You fritter and waste the hours in an offhand way.
Kicking around on a piece of ground in your hometown,
Waiting for someone or something to show you the way.

Tired of lying in the sunshine, staying home to watch the rain.
And you are young and life is long and there is time to kill today.
And then one day you find ten years have got behind you.
No one told you when to run. You missed the starting gun.

And you run, you run to catch up with the sun, but it's sinking
And racing around to come up behind you again.
The sun is the same in a relative way, but you're older,
Shorter of breath, and one day closer to death.

Ev'ry year is getting shorter, never seem to find the time.
Plans that either come to naught or a half page of scribbled lines.
Hanging on in quiet desperation is the English way.
The time is gone, the song is over. Thought I'd something more to say.

Time for Me to Fly

Words and Music by Kevin Cronin

recorded by REO Speedwagon

I've been around for you,
Been up and down for you,
But I just can't get any relief.
I've swallowed my pride for you,
Lived and lied for you,
But you still make me feel like a thief.

You got me stealin' your love away 'cause you never give it;
Peelin' the years away and we can't relive it.
I make you laugh, and you make me cry.
I believe it's time for me to fly.

You said we'd work it out.
You said that you had no doubt
That deep down we were really in love.
But I'm tired of holding on
To a feeling I know is gone.
I do believe that I've had enough.

I've had enough of the falseness of a worn-out relation,
Enough of the jealousy and the intoleration.
I make you laugh, and you make me cry.
I believe it's time for me to fly.

Time for me to fly.
I've got to set myself free.
Time for me to fly.
That's just how it's got to be.
I know it hurts to say good-bye,
But it's time for me to fly.
It's time for me to fly.

Tonight's the Night
(Gonna Be Alright)

Words and Music by Rod Stewart

recorded by Rod Stewart

Stay away from my window;
Stay away from my back door, too.
Disconnect the telephone line;
Relax, baby, and draw the blind.

Kick off your shoes and sit right down
And loosen up that pretty French gown.
Let me pour you a good long drink;
Ooh, baby, don't you hesitate.

Refrain:
'Cause
Tonight's the night;
It's gonna be alright.
'Cause I love you, girl;
Ain't nobody gonna stop us now.

Come on angel, my heart's on fire;
Don't deny your man's desire.
You'd be a fool to stop this tide;
Spread your wings and let me come inside.

Refrain

Don't say a word, my virgin child;
Just let your inhibitions run wild.
The secret is about to unfold
Upstairs before the night's too old.

Refrain

Tumbling Dice

Words and Music by Mick Jagger and Keith Richards

recorded by The Rolling Stones

Women think I'm tasty
But they're always trying to waste me
And make me burn the candle right down,
But baby, baby, I don't need no jewels in
my crown.

'Cause all you women
Is low down gamblers,
Cheatin' like I don't know how,
But baby, baby, there's fever in the funk
house now.

This low down bitchin' got my poor
feet a-itchin',
You know, you know the deuce is still wild.
Baby, baby I can't stay, you got to roll me
And call me the tumblin' dice.

Always in a hurry,
I never stop to worry,
Don't you see the time flashin' by.
Honey, got no money,
I'm all sixes and sevens and nines.

Say now, baby, I'm the rank outsider,
You can be my partner in crime.
But baby, I can't stay,
You got to roll me and call me tumblin' dice.

Twice:
Oh, my, me, me, I'm the lone crap shooter,
Playin' the field every night.
Baby, can't stay, you got to roll me
And call me tumblin' dice.
Got to roll me
And call me the tumblin' dice.

Turn Me Loose

Words and Music by Paul Dean and Duke Reno

recorded by Loverboy

I was born to run, I was born to dream.
The craziest boy you've ever seen.
I've gotta do it my way, or no way at all.
And I was here to please, I'm even on
  my knees,
Making love to whoever I please.
I've gotta do it my way, or no way at all.

And then you came around, tried to tie me
  down.
I was such a clown.
You had to have it your way, or no way at all.
But I've had all I can take, I can't take it
  no more.
I'm gonna pack my bags and fly it my way,
Or no way at all.

Refrain:
So why don't you turn me loose?
Turn me loose. Turn me loose.
I've gotta do it my way, or no way at all.
Why don't you turn me loose?
Turn me loose. Turn me loose.
I've gotta do it my way.
I wanna fly.

I'm here to please, I'm even on my knees,
Making love to whoever I please.
I've gotta do it my way,
I've gotta do it my way.
And when you come around, you tried to tie
  me down.
I was such a clown.
You had to have it your way,
Well, I'm sayin', no way.

Refrain

So why don't you turn me loose?
Turn me loose. Turn me loose.
I've gotta do it my way, or no way at all.
Why don't you turn me loose?
Turn me loose. Turn me loose.
I've gotta do it my way,
I've gotta do it my way.
Why don't you turn me loose?
Turn me loose. Turn me loose.
I've gotta do it my way.
I wanna fly.

Seven Times:
Turn me loose.

Turn! Turn! Turn!
(To Everything There Is a Season)

Words from the Book of Ecclesiastes
Adaptation and Music by Pete Seeger

recorded by The Byrds

To everything (turn, turn, turn)
There is a season (turn, turn, turn)
And a time for every purpose under heaven.
A time to be born, a time to die
A time to plant, a time to reap;
A time to kill, a time to heal;
A time to laugh, a time to weep.

To everything (turn, turn, turn)
There is a season (turn, turn, turn)
And a time for every purpose under heaven.

A time to build up,
A time to break down;
A time to dance, a time to mourn;
A time to cast away stones,
A time to gather stones together.

To everything (turn, turn, turn)
There is a season (turn, turn, turn)
And a time for every purpose under heaven.

A time of love, a time of hate;
A time of war, a time of peace;
A time you may embrace,
A time to refrain from embracing.

To everything (turn, turn, turn)
There is a season (turn, turn, turn)
And a time for every purpose under heaven.

Two Out of Three Ain't Bad

Words and Music by Jim Steinman

recorded by Meat Loaf

Baby, we can talk all night,
But that ain't getting us nowhere.
I've told you ev'rything I possibly can.
There's nothing left inside of here.
And maybe you can cry all night,
But that'll never change the way that I feel.
The snow is really piling up outside,
I wish you wouldn't make me leave here.
I poured it on and I poured it out.
I tried to show you just how much I care.
I'm tired of words and I'm too hoarse
   to shout.
But you've been cold to me so long,
I'm crying icicles instead of tears,
And all I can do is keep on telling you

I want you, I need you,
But there ain't no way I'm ever gonna
   love you.
Now don't be sad, 'cause two out of three
   ain't bad.
Now don't be sad, 'cause two out of three
   ain't bad.

You'll never find your gold on a sandy beach.
You'll never drill for oil on a city street.
I know you're looking for a ruby in a
   mountain of rocks,
But there ain't no Coupe de Ville hiding at
   the bottom of a Crackerjack box.
I can't lie, I can't tell you that I'm something
   I'm not.
No matter how I try, I'll never be able to give
   you something,
Something that I just haven't got.

Well, there's only one girl that I will
   ever love,
And that was so many years ago.
And though I know I'll never get her out of
   my heart,
She never loved me back, ooh, I know.
Well, I remember how she left me on a
   stormy night.
Oh, she kissed me and got out of our bed.
And though I pleaded and I begged her not
   to walk out that door,
She packed her bags and turned right away.
And she kept on telling me, she kept on
   telling me,
She kept on telling me,

Twice:
I want you, I need you,
But there ain't no way I'm ever gonna
   love you.
Now don't be sad, 'cause two out of three
   ain't bad.

Now don't be sad, 'cause two out of three
   ain't bad.

Baby, we can talk all night,
But that ain't getting us nowhere.

Walk on the Wild Side

Words and Music by Lou Reed

recorded by Lou Reed

Holly came from Miami, FLA.
Hitch-hiked her way across the USA.
Plucked her eyebrows on the way,
Shaved her legs and then he was a she.
She says, "Hey, babe, take a walk on the
   wild side."
I said, "Hey, babe, take a walk on the
   wild side."

And the colored girls go,
Doo, doo doo, doo doo, doo doo doo.
Doo, doo doo, doo doo, doo doo doo...

Candy came from out on the island.
In the back room she was ev'rybody's
   darlin'.
But she never lost her head,
Even when she was giving head.
She said, "Hey, babe, take a walk on the
   wild side."
I said, "Hey, babe, take a walk on the
   wild side."

Little Joe never once gave it away.
Ev'rybody had to pay and pay.
A hustle here and a hustle there.
New York City is the place where they said,
"Hey, babe, take a walk on the wild side."
I said, "Hey, babe, take a walk on the
   wild side."

Sugar Plum Fairy came and hit the streets,
Lookin' for soul food and a place to eat.
Went to the Apollo,
You should have seen 'em go, go, go.
They said, "Hey, babe, take a walk on the
   wild side."
I said, "Hey, babe, take a walk on the
   wild side."

Jackie is just speedin' away.
Thought she was James Dean for a day.
Then I guess she had to crash.
Valium would have helped that bash.
She said, "Hey, babe, take a walk on the
   wild side."
I said, "Hey, babe, take a walk on the
   wild side."

And the colored girls go,
Doo, doo doo, doo doo, doo doo doo.
Doo, doo doo, doo doo, doo doo doo...

Walk This Way

Words and Music by Steven Tyler and Joe Perry

recorded by Aerosmith

Back stroke lover always hidin' 'neath
   the covers
Till I talked to your daddy, he say.
He said, "You ain't seen nothin'
Till you're down on a muffin,
Then you're sure to be a changin'
   your ways."
I meet a cheerleader, was a real young
   bleeder, oh,
The times I could reminisce;
'Cause the best things of lovin'
With her sister and her cousin
Only started with a little kiss.
Spoken:
Like this.

See-saw swinger with the boys in the school
And your feet flyin' up in the air,
Singin' "Hey, diddle, diddle,"
With your kitty in the middle of the swing
Like you didn't care.
So I took a big glance
At the high school dance
With a missy who was ready to play.
Was it me she was foolin'
'Cause she knew what she was doin',
When I knowed love was here to stay,
Spoken:
When she told me to,
Sung:
Walk this way, talk this way.

School girl sweeties with a classy,
   kind-a sassy
Little skirts climbin' up to their knees;
There was three young ladies in the school
   gym locker
When I noticed they was lookin' at me.
I was a high school loser,
Never made it with a lady
Till the boys told me somethin' I missed.
Then my next door neighbor with a daughter
   had a favor,
So I gave her just a little kiss
Spoken:
Like this.

See-saw swinger with the boys in the school
And your feet flyin' up in the air,
Singin' "Hey, diddle, diddle,"
With your kitty in the middle of the swing
Like you didn't care.
So I took a big glance
At the high school dance
With a missy who was ready to play.
Was it me she was foolin'
'Cause she knew what she was doin'
When she taught me how to
Walk this way.
Spoken:
When she told me to,
Sung:
Walk this way, talk this way,
Spoken:
And just gimme a kiss, like this.

Walking in Memphis

Words and Music by Marc Cohn

recorded by Marc Cohn

Put on my blue suede shoes
And I boarded the plane.
Touched down in the land of the Delta Blues
In the middle of the pouring rain.
W.C. Handy—won't you look down over me?
Yeah, I got a first class ticket,
But I'm as blue as a boy can be.

Then I'm walking in Memphis,
Was walking with my feet ten feet off of
    Beale.
Walking in Memphis,
But do I really feel the way I feel?

Saw the ghost of Elvis
On Union Avenue.
Followed him up to the gates of Graceland,
Then I watched him walk right through.
Now security they did not see him,
They just hovered 'round his tomb.
But there's a pretty little thing
Waiting for the King
Down in the Jungle Room.

When I was walking in Memphis,
I was walking with my feet ten feet off of
    Beale.
Walking in Memphis,
But do I really feel the way I feel?

They've got catfish on the table.
They've got gospel in the air.
And Reverend Green be glad to see you
When you haven't got a prayer.
But, boy, you've got a prayer in Memphis.

Now Muriel plays piano
Every Friday at The Hollywood.
And they brought me down to see her.
And they asked me if I would
Do a little number,
And I sang with all my might.
She said, "Tell me, are you a Christian
    child?"
And I said, "Ma'am, I am tonight."

Walking in Memphis,
Was walking with my feet ten feet off of
    Beale.
Walking in Memphis,
But do I really feel the way I feel?

Walking in Memphis,
I was walking with my feet ten feet off of
    Beale.
Walking in Memphis,
But do I really feel the way I feel?

Put on my blue suede shoes
And I boarded the plane.
Touched down in the land of the Delta Blues
In the middle of the pouring rain.
Touched down in the land of the Delta Blues
In the middle of the pouring rain.

We Gotta Get Out of This Place

Words and Music by Barry Mann and Cynthia Weil

recorded by The Animals

In this dirty old part of the city
Where the sun refuse to shine,
People tell me there ain't no use in tryin'.
My little girl, you're so young and pretty.
And one thing I know is true:
You'll be dead before your time is through.
See my daddy in bed. He's dyin'.
You know, his hair is turning grey.
He's been working and slaving his life away.

Gotta work.
Work.
We gotta work.
Work, work, work, work.

We gotta get out of this place
If it's the last thing we ever do.
We gotta get out of this place.
Girl, there's a better life for me and you.

We Will Rock You

Words and Music by Brian May

recorded by Queen

Buddy you're a boy
Make a big noise
Playin' in the street
Gonna be a big man someday.
You got mud on yo' face
You big disgrace
Kickin' your can all over the place.
Singin' we will, we will rock you.
We will, we will rock you.

Buddy you're a young man,
Hard man
Shootin' in the street
Gonna take on the world some day.
You got mud on yo' face
You big disgrace
Wavin' your banner all over the place.
Singin' we will, we will rock you.
We will, we will rock you.

Buddy you're an old man,
Poor man
Pleadin' with your eyes
Gonna make you some peace someday.
You got mud on yo' face
You big disgrace
Somebody better put you back into your place
Singin' we will, we will rock you,
We will, we will rock you.
We will, we will rock you.

Wheel in the Sky

Words and Music by Robert Fleischman, Neal Schon and Diane Valory

recorded by Journey

Winter is here again, oh, Lord.
Haven't been home in a year or more.
I hope she holds on a little longer.
Sent a letter on a long summer day
Made of silver, not of clay.
I've been runnin' down this dusty road.

Refrain:
The wheel in the sky keeps on turnin'.
I don't know where I'll be tomorrow.
Wheel in the sky keeps on turnin'.

I've been tryin' to make it home.
Got to make it before too long.
I can't take this very much longer, no.
I'm stranded in the sleet and rain.
Don't think I'm ever gonna make it
    home again.
The mornin' sun is risin', it's kissin' the day.

Refrain

The wheel in the sky keeps on turnin'.
I don't know where I'll be tomorrow.
Wheel in the sky keeps me yearnin'.
I don't know, I don't know, I don't know.

The wheel in the sky keeps on turnin'.
I don't know where I'll be tomorrow.
Wheel in the sky keeps on turnin'.
I don't know, I don't know, I don't know.

Wheel in the sky keeps on turnin'.
I don't know where I'll be tomorrow.
The wheel in the sky keeps on turnin'.
Wheel in the sky keeps on turnin'.

A Whiter Shade of Pale

Words and Music by Keith Reid and Gary Brooker

recorded by Procol Harum

We skipped the light fandago,
Turned cartwheels 'cross the floor;
I was feeling kind of seasick,
The crowd called out for more.
The room was humming harder
As the ceiling flew away.
When we called for another drink
The waiter brought a tray.

Refrain:
And so it was that later
As the miller told his tale,
That her face, at first just ghostly,
Turned a whiter shade of pale.

She said, "I'm home on shore leave,"
Through in truth we were at sea;
So I took her by the looking glass
And forced her to agree.
Saying, "You must be the mermaid
Who took Neptune for a ride,"
But she smiled at me so sadly
That my anger straightaway died.

Refrain

She said, "There is no reason,
And the truth is plain to see,"
But I wandered through my playing cards
And would not let her be
One of sixteen vestal virgins
Who were leaving for the coast.
And although my eyes were open
They might just as well been closed.

Refrain

Windy

Words and Music by Ruthann Friedman

recorded by The Association

Who's peekin' out from under a stairway,
Calling a name that's lighter than air?
Who's bendin' down to give me a rainbow?
Ev'ryone knows it's Windy.

Who's trippin' down the streets of the city,
Smilin' at ev'rybody she sees?
Who's reachin' out to capture a moment?
Ev'ryone knows it's Windy.

Refrain:
And Windy has stormy eyes
That flash at the sound of lies.
And Windy has wings to fly
Above the clouds, above the clouds,
Above the clouds, above the clouds.

Repeat Refrain

Repeat Verse 2

Woman from Tokyo

Words and Music by Ritchie Blackmore, Ian Gillan, Roger Glover, Jon Lord and Ian Paice

recorded by Deep Purple

Fly into the risin' sun.
Faces smilin' every one. Yeah!
She is a whole new tradition. Ow!
I feel it in my heart!

Refrain:
My woman from Tokyo.
She makes me see.
My woman from Tokyo.
She's so good to me.

Talk about her like a queen,
Dancing in an eastern dream.
Yeah, she makes me feel like a river, ow!
That carries me away.

Refrain

Risin' from the neon gloom,
Shinin' like a crazy moon.
Yeah, she tuns me on like a fire.
Ow! I get high!

Refrain

When I'm at home an' I, I just don't belong.

So far away from the garden we love.
She is what moves in the soul of a dove.
Soon I shall see just how black was my night,
When we're alone in her city of light.
Oooo...

Refrain

Wonderful Tonight

Words and Music by Eric Clapton

recorded by Eric Clapton

It's late in the evening; she's wondering what clothes to wear.
She puts on her makeup and brushes her long blonde hair.
And then she asks me, "Do I look all right?"
And I say, "Yes, you look wonderful tonight."

We go to a party, and everyone turns to see
This beautiful lady is walking around with me.
And then she asks me, "Do you feel all right?"
And I say, "Yes, I feel wonderful tonight."

I feel wonderful because I see the love light in your eyes.
Then the wonder of it all is that you just don't realize
How much I love you.

It's time to go home now, and I've got an aching head.
So I give her the car keys, and she helps me to bed.
And then I tell her, as I turn out the light, I say,
"My darling, you are wonderful tonight.
Oh, my darling, you are wonderful tonight."

Working for the Weekend

Words and Music by Paul Dean, Matthew Frenette and Michael Reno

recorded by Loverboy

Ev'ryone's watchin' to see what you will do.
Ev'ryone's lookin' at you, ooo.
Ev'ryone's wonderin', will you come out tonight.
Ev'ryone's tryin' to get it right, get it right.

Refrain:
Ev'rybody's workin' for the weekend.
Ev'rybody wants a new romance.
Ev'rybody's goin' off the deep end.
Ev'rybody needs a second chance, oh.
You want a piece of my heart.
You better start from the start.
You wanna be in the show.
Come on, baby, let's go!

Ev'ryone's lookin' to see if it was you.
Ev'ryone wants you to come through.
Ev'ryone's hopin' it'll all work out.
Ev'ryone's waitin' to hold it out.

Refrain

Twice:
You want a piece of my heart.
You better start from the start.
You wanna be in the show.
Come on, baby, let's go!

Wouldn't It Be Nice

Words and Music by Brian Wilson, Tony Asher and Mike Love

recorded by The Beach Boys

Wouldn't it be nice if we were older,
Then we wouldn't have to wait so long.
And wouldn't it be nice to live together
In the kind of world where we'd belong.
Though it's gonna make it that much better
When we can say goodnight and stay together.

Wouldn't it be nice if we could wake up
In the morning when the day is new,
And after that to spend the day together,
Hold each other close the whole night through.
The happy times together we'd been spending,
I wish that ev'ry kiss was never ending.
Oh, wouldn't it be nice.

Well, maybe if we think and wish
And hope and pray, it might come true.
Baby, then there wouldn't be
A single thing we couldn't do.
We could be married, and then we'd be happy.
Oh, wouldn't it be nice.

You Ain't Seen Nothin' Yet

Words and Music by Randy Bachman

recorded by Bachman-Turner Overdrive

I met a devil woman,
She took my heart away.
She said I had it comin' to me,
And I wanted it that way.
She said that:

Refrain:
Any love is good lovin',
So I took what I could get.
Yes, I took what I could get.
And then she looked at me with those big brown eyes and she said:
"You ain't seen nothin' yet.
B-b-b-baby, you just ain't never gonna forget baby.
Ya know, ya know, ya know,
You know, you know you just ain't seen nothin' yet."

And now I'm feelin' better
'Cause I found out for sure.
She took me to her doctor
And he told me of a cure.
He said that:

Refrain

You Give Love a Bad Name

Words and Music by Desmond Child, Jon Bon Jovi and Richie Sambora

recorded by Bon Jovi

An angel's smile is what you sell.
You promise me heaven, then put me through hell.
Chains of love got a hold on me.
When passion's a prison, you can't break free.

Refrain:
Oh you're a loaded gun. Yeah.
Oh, there's nowhere to run.
No one can save me, the damage is done.
Shot through the heart and you're to blame.
You give love a bad name.
I play my part and you play your game.
You give love a bad name,
Hey, you give love a bad name.

You paint your smile on your lips.
Blood red nails on your finger tips.
A school boy's dream, you act so shy.
Your very first kiss was your first kiss goodbye.

You May Be Right

Words and Music by Billy Joel

recorded by Billy Joel

Friday night I crashed your party,
Saturday I said I'm sorry,
Sunday came and trashed me out again.
I was only having fun,
Wasn't hurting anyone,
And we all enjoyed the weekend for a
    change.

I've been stranded in the combat zone,
I walked through Bedford Stuy alone,
Even rode my motorcycle in the rain.
And you told me not to drive,
But I made it home alive,
So you said that only proves that I'm insane.

Refrain 1:
You may be right.
I may be crazy.
But it just may be a lunatic you're
    looking for.
Turn out the light,
Don't try to save me.
You may be wrong for all I know
But you may be right.

Well, remember how I found you you there,
Alone in your electric chair,
I told you dirty jokes until you smiled.
You were lonely for a man.
I said, "Take me as I am,"
'Cause you might enjoy some madness for
    awhile.

Now think of all the years you tried to
Find someone to satisfy you.
I might be as crazy as you say.
If I'm crazy, then it's true,
That it's all because of you,
And you wouldn't want me any other way.

Refrain 2:
You may be right.
I may be crazy.
But it just may be a lunatic you're
    looking for.
It's too late to fight,
It's too late to change me.
You may be wrong for all I know
But you may be right.

Refrain 1

You may be wrong but you may be right.

You Really Got Me

Words and Music by Ray Davies

recorded by The Kinks, Van Halen

Girl, you really got me going.
You got me so I don't know what I'm doing.
Yeah, you really got me now.
You got me so I can't sleep at night.
Yeah, you really got me now.
You got me so I don't know what I'm doing.
Oh, yeah, you really got me now.
You got me so I can't sleep at night.
You really got me.
You really got me.
You really got me.

See, don't ever set me free.
I always wanna be by your side.
Girl, you really got me now.
You got me so I can't sleep at night.
Yeah, you really got me now.
You got me so I don't know what I'm doing.
Oh, yeah, you really got me now.
You got me so I can't sleep at night.
You really got me.
You really got me.
You really got me.

Repeat Verse 2

You're My Best Friend

Words and Music by John Deacon

recorded by Queen

Ooh, you make me live;
Whatever this world can give to me.
It's you, you're all I see.
Ooh, you make me live now, honey,
Ooh, you make me live.

Ooh, you're the best friend that I ever had.
I've been with you such a long time,
You're my sunshine and I want you to know,
That my feelings are true,
I really love you.

Refrain:
Oh, you're my best friend.
Ooh, you make me live.
Ooh, I've been wandering 'round,
But I still come back to you.
In rain or shine you've stood by me, girl.
I'm happy at home,
You're my best friend.

Ooh, you make me live
Whenever this world is cruel to me.
I got you to help me forgive.
Ooh, you make me live now, honey,
Ooh, you make me live.

Ooh, you're the first one when things turn out bad.
You know I'll never be lonely,
You're my only one and I love the things,
I really love the things that you do.

Refrain

Ooh, ooh, you're my best friend.
Ooh, you make me live.
Ooh, you're my best friend.

Ziggy Stardust

Words and Music by David Bowie

recorded by David Bowie

Ziggy played guitar,
Jamming good with Weird and Gilly,
The spiders from Mars.
He played it left hand but made it too far,
Became the special man,
Then we were Ziggy's band.

Ziggy really sang,
Screwed-up eyes and screwed-down hairdo
Like some cat from Japan.
He could lick 'em by smiling,
He could leave 'em to hang.
Came on so loaded, well-hung, and snow-white tan.

So where were the spiders
While the fly tried to break our balls
With just the beer light to guide us.
So we bitched about his fans,
And should we crush his sweet hands?

Ziggy played for time,
Jiving us that we were voodoo.
The kid was just crass,
He was a nazz with God-given ass.
He took it all too far,
But boy, could he play guitar.

Making love with his ego,
Ziggy sucked up into his mind
Like a leper messiah.
When the kids had killed the man
I had to break up the band.

Oh, yeah.
Oh, Ziggy played guitar.

Young Americans

Words and Music by David Bowie

recorded by David Bowie

They pulled in just behind the bridge,
He lays her down. He frowns,
"Gee, my life's a funny thing.
Am I still too young?"
He kissed her then and there;
She took his ring, took his babies
It took him minutes, took her nowhere.
Heaven knows, she'd have taken anything.

All night she wants the young American.
Young American, young American,
She wants the young American.
All right, she wants the young American.

Scanning life through the picture window,
She finds her slinky vagabond.
He coughs as he passes her Ford Mustang,
But heaven forbid, she'll take anything
But the freak and his type, all for nothing.
Misses a step and cuts his hand,
Showing nothing, he swoops like a song.
She cries, "Where have all Papa's heroes
    gone?"

All night she wants the young American.
Young American, young American,
She wants the young American.
All right, she wants the young American.

All the way from Washington,
Her breadwinner begs off the bathroom
    floor.
We live for just these twenty years
Till we have to die for the fifty more.

All night he wants the young American.
Young American, young American,
He wants the young American.
All right, he wants the young American.

Do you remember your President Nixon?
Do you remember the bills you have to pay,
Or even yesterday?

Have you been an un-American?
Just you and your idol singing falsetto
'bout leather, leather everywhere, and
Not a myth left from the ghetto.
Well, well, well, would you carry a razor
In case, just in case of depression?
Sit on your hands on a bus of survivors
Blushing at all the Afro-Sheilas.
Ain't that close to love?
Well, ain't that poster love?
Well, it ain't that Barbie doll.
Her heart's been broken just like you have.

All night, want the young American.
Young American, young American,
You want the young American.
All right, you want the young American.

You ain't a pimp, and you ain't a hustler.
A pimp's got a Cadi and a lady's got a Chrysler.
Black's got respect, and white's got his Soul Train.
Mama's got cramps, and look at your hands ache.
(I heard the news today, oh boy.)
I gotta suite and you got defeat.
Ain't there a man who can say no more?
And ain't there a woman I can sock on the jaw?
And ain't there a child I can hold without judging?
Ain't there a pen that will write before they die?
Ain't you proud that you've still got faces?
Ain't there one damn song that can make me break down and cry?

All night I want the young American.
Young American, young American,
I want the young American.
All right, I want the young American.

Artist Index

The Hollies
33 Bus Stop
121 Long Cool Woman (In a
Black Dress)

Billy Idol
46 Cradle of Love

J.J. Jackson
34 But It's Alright

Billy Joel
10 Allentown
15 Baby Grand
106 It's Still Rock and Roll to Me
137 Only the Good Die Young
210 You May Be Right

Elton John
26 The Bitch Is Back
54 Don't Let the Sun Go Down
on Me
144 Philadelphia Freedom

Janis Joplin
126 Me and Bobby McGee
145 Piece of My Heart

Journey
14 Anytime
201 Wheel in the Sky

Kansas
38 Carry On Wayward Son
61 Dust in the Wind
146 Point of Know Return

The Kinks
8 All Day and All of the Night
211 You Really Got Me

John Lennon
101 Instant Karma

Huey Lewis and The News
83 Heart and Soul

Loverboy
193 Turn Me Loose
206 Working for the Weekend

Lynyrd Skynyrd
36 Call Me the Breeze

Meat Loaf
140 Paradise by the Dashboard Light
195 Two Out of Three Ain't Bad

John Cougar Mellencamp
94 Hurts So Good

The Moody Blues
117 Legend of a Mind
134 Nights in White Satin
148 Question
175 The Story in Your Eyes

Mountain
129 Mississippi Queen

Nazareth
80 Hair of the Dog
122 Love Hurts

Alan Parsons Project
68 Eye in the Sky

Tom Petty
100 I Won't Back Down
115 Learning to Fly
160 Runnin' Down a Dream

Tom Petty and The Heartbreakers
31 Breakdown
52 Don't Do Me Like That
152 Refugee

Pink Floyd
29 Brain Damage
32 Breathe
130 Money
189 Time

The Police
55 Don't Stand So Close to Me
65 Every Breath You Take
66 Every Little Thing She Does
Is Magic
107 King of Pain
127 Message in a Bottle
158 Roxanne

The Pretenders
30 Brass in Pocket

Procol Harum
202 A Whiter Shade of Pale

Queen
13 Another One Bites the Dust
47 Crazy Little Thing Called Love
200 We Will Rock You
212 You're My Best Friend

Bonnie Raitt
172 Something to Talk About

Lou Reed
196 Walk on the Wild Side

REO Speedwagon
155 Ridin' the Storm Out
190 Time for Me to Fly

The Rolling Stones
11 Angie
24 Beast of Burden
64 Emotional Rescue
81 Happy
105 It's Only Rock 'n' Roll
(But I Like It)
128 Miss You
164 Shattered
166 She's So Cold
174 Start Me Up
192 Tumbling Dice

Todd Rundgren
89 Hello, It's Me

Bob Seger
163 Shakedown

The Shadows of Knight
77 Gloria

Steppenwolf
147 The Pusher

Rod Stewart
49 Da Ya Think I'm Sexy
73 Forever Young
124 Maggie May
191 Tonight's the Night (Gonna Be
Alright)

Sting
74 Fortress Around Your Heart

Styx
27 Blue Collar Man (Long Nights)
44 Come Sail Away
71 Fooling Yourself (The Angry
Young Man)

Sugarloaf
79 Green-Eyed Lady

Supertramp
58 Dreamer
76 Give a Little Bit
120 The Logical Song
186 Take the Long Way Home

Survivor
69 Eye of the Tiger

Sweet
22 Ballroom Blitz

Them
77 Gloria

.38 Special
39 Caught Up in You
157 Rockin' into the Night

Tommy Tutone
63 867-5309/Jenny

Songwriter Index

Mick Jones
43 Cold as Ice
93 Hot Blooded

Seth Justman
40 Centerfold

James Keller
63 867-5309/Jenny

Holly Knight
123 Love Is a Battlefield

Mark Knopfler
131 Money for Nothing
180 Sultans of Swing

George Kooymans
149 Radar Love

Kris Kristofferson
126 Me and Bobby McGee

Corky Laing
129 Mississippi Queen

John Lennon
18 Back in the U.S.S.R.
45 Come Together
50 Day Tripper
60 Drive My Car
70 Fame
82 A Hard Day's Night
97 I Feel Fine
101 Instant Karma
108 Lady Madonna
153 Revolution

Mike Levine
113 Lay It on the Line

Marcy Levy
112 Lay Down Sally

Kerry Livgren
38 Carry On Wayward Son
61 Dust in the Wind

Jon Lord
169 Smoke on the Water
204 Woman from Tokyo

Mike Love
35 California Girls
207 Wouldn't It Be Nice

Jeff Lynne
51 Don't Bring Me Down
67 Evil Woman
100 I Won't Back Down
115 Learning to Fly
160 Runnin' Down a Dream
185 Sweet Talkin' Woman

Barry Mann
199 We Gotta Get Out of This Place

Bob Marley
99 I Shot the Sheriff

Nicholas Mason
189 Time

Brian May
200 We Will Rock You

Dan McCafferty
80 Hair of the Dog

Paul McCartney
18 Back in the U.S.S.R.
45 Come Together
50 Day Tripper
60 Drive My Car
82 A Hard Day's Night
97 I Feel Fine
108 Lady Madonna
153 Revolution

James McCarty
138 Over Under Sideways Down

Roger McGuinn
62 Eight Miles High

Christine McVie
56 Don't Stop

John Mellencamp
94 Hurts So Good

Freddie Mercury
47 Crazy Little Thing Called Love

Gil Moore
113 Lay It on the Line

Van Morrison
77 Gloria

Stevie Nicks
59 Dreams
110 Landslide
154 Rhiannon

Rick Nielsen
182 Surrender

Robert Nix
170 So into You

Ian Paice
169 Smoke on the Water
204 Woman from Tokyo

Felix Pappalardi
129 Mississippi Queen
176 Strange Brew

Alan Parsons
68 Eye in the Sky

Joe Perry
17 Back in the Saddle
197 Walk This Way

Jim Peterik
39 Caught Up in You
69 Eye of the Tiger
157 Rockin' into the Night

Tom Petty
31 Breakdown
52 Don't Do Me Like That
100 I Won't Back Down
115 Learning to Fly
152 Refugee
160 Runnin' Down a Dream

J.C. Phillips
79 Green-Eyed Lady

Martin Quittenton
124 Maggie May

Trevor Rabin
116 Leave It
139 Owner of a Lonely Heart

Jerry Ragovoy
145 Piece of My Heart

David Rea
129 Mississippi Queen

Lou Reed
196 Walk on the Wild Side

Keith Reid
202 A Whiter Shade of Pale

Keith Relf
138 Over Under Sideways Down

Michael "Duke" Reno
193 Turn Me Loose
206 Working for the Weekend

Keith Richards
11 Angie
24 Beast of Burden
64 Emotional Rescue
81 Happy
105 It's Only Rock 'n' Roll
    (But I Like It)
128 Miss You
164 Shattered
166 She's So Cold
174 Start Me Up
192 Tumbling Dice

Gary Richrath
155 Ridin' the Storm Out

David Riordan
79 Green-Eyed Lady

Billy Roberts
91 Hey Joe

Paul Rodgers
9 All Right Now

Donald Roeser
53 Don't Fear the Reaper
78 Godzilla

Greg Rolie
14 Anytime

Todd Rundgren
89 Hello, It's Me

Mike Rutherford
102 Invisible Touch
109 Land of Confusion

Richie Sambora
20 Bad Medicine
209 You Give Love a Bad Name

Ralph Santer
113 Lay It on the Line

Kevin Savigar
73 Forever Young

Neal Schon
14 Anytime
201 Wheel in the Sky

Eddie Schwartz
92 Hit Me with Your Best Shot

Ronnie Scott
103 It's a Heartache

Pete Seeger
194 Turn! Turn! Turn! (To Everything
      There Is a Season)

Bob Seger
86 Heartache Tonight
163 Shakedown

Tommy Shaw
27 Blue Collar Man (Long Nights)
71 Fooling Yourself (The Angry
      Young Man)

Roger Silver
14 Anytime

Neal Smith
162 School's Out

Robert Gary Smith
157 Rockin' into the Night

Joe South
95 Hush

John David Souther
84 The Heart of the Matter
86 Heartache Tonight
133 New Kid in Town

Chris Squire
116 Leave It
139 Owner of a Lonely Heart

Robert Steinhardt
146 Point of Know Return

Jim Steinman
140 Paradise by the Dashboard Light
195 Two Out of Three Ain't Bad

Rod Stewart
49 Da Ya Think I'm Sexy
73 Forever Young
124 Maggie May
191 Tonight's the Night (Gonna Be
      Alright)

Stephen Stills
178 Suite: Judy Blue Eyes

Sting (G.M. Sumner)
55 Don't Stand So Close to Me
65 Every Breath You Take
66 Every Little Thing She Does
      Is Magic
74 Fortress Around Your Heart
107 King of Pain
127 Message in a Bottle
131 Money for Nothing
158 Roxanne

Frank Sullivan
39 Caught Up in You
69 Eye of the Tiger
157 Rockin' into the Night

G.M. Sumner *(see Sting)*

Darrell Sweet
80 Hair of the Dog

Bernie Taupin
26 The Bitch Is Back
54 Don't Let the Sun Go Down
      on Me
144 Philadelphia Freedom

George Terry
112 Lay Down Sally

Ray Thomas
117 Legend of a Mind

Peter Townshend
96 I Can See for Miles
125 The Magic Bus
132 My Generation

Pierre Tubbs
34 But It's Alright

Charles Turner
119 Let It Ride

Steven Tyler
17 Back in the Saddle
57 Dream On
111 Last Child
184 Sweet Emotion
197 Walk This Way

Jim Vallance
88 Heaven
104 It's Only Love
159 Run to You

Ross Vallory
14 Anytime

Diane Valory
201 Wheel in the Sky

Steve Walsh
146 Point of Know Return

Roger Waters
29 Brain Damage
32 Breathe
130 Money
189 Time

Cynthia Weil
199 We Gotta Get Out of This Place

David Werner
46 Cradle of Love

Leslie West
129 Mississippi Queen

Jamie West-Oram
136 One Thing Leads to Another

John Wetton
87 Heat of the Moment

Brad Whitford
111 Last Child

Jerry Williams
161 Running on Faith

Ann Wilson
23 Barracuda
48 Crazy on You

More Collections from the Lyric Library

The Lyric Library lets you bring more completeness and accuracy to your song repertoire. Rediscover a nearly forgotten gem, wallow in nostalgia, or browse through examples of great songwriting and enjoy the words as poetry set to music. Each jam-packed collection features complete lyrics to over 200 songs.

BROADWAY VOLUME I
00240201 $14.95

BROADWAY VOLUME II
00240205 $14.95

CHRISTMAS
00240206 $14.95

CLASSIC ROCK
00240183 $14.95

CONTEMPORARY CHRISTIAN
00240184 $14.95

COUNTRY
00240204 $14.95

EARLY ROCK 'N' ROLL
00240203 $14.95

LOVE SONGS
00240186 $14.95

POP/ROCK BALLADS
00240187 $14.95

See our website for a complete contents list for each volume:
www.halleonard.com

FOR MORE INFORMATION, SEE YOUR LOCAL MUSIC DEALER,
OR WRITE TO:

HAL•LEONARD®
CORPORATION

7777 W. BLUEMOUND RD. P.O. BOX 13819 MILWAUKEE, WI 53213

Prices, contents and availability subject to change without notice.